SAVVY

SAVVY

When I grow Up I'm Going To Be Rich!

The Simple Secrets To Build Wealth And Live Your Best Life

By Michael Munsterman

This book is dedicated to anyone that
has ever had that voice in their mind
or in their heart saying

"I AM MEANT FOR MORE THAN THIS!"

My hope is that this book gives you the courage to jump, keep jumping, or jump higher and harder than you currently are!

Content

Introduction

In the Beginning

The Beginning

I was seven years old when my mom and my stepdad sat me down on the bed and said, "Your father died this morning. He was in a bad accident, and he's in heaven now." I shrieked in horror, in horror of the moment, in horror of the pain in my chest, and in horror of not being able to breathe. Mostly I just cried out because I needed my best friend to bust through the door and sweep me up from this nightmare.

My dad, Joe, worked for the Missouri State Highway Department. He was the perfect mix of both my grandmother and my grandfather. He was hard working, compassionate, and entrepreneurial. Not only did he work for the state, but he also had his own little side hustles to earn extra money. Joe Munsterman was just a good ole boy who wore plain blue jeans and cowboy boots. He had a great big smile, and everyone liked him. He articulated his thoughts clearly and had a bright future that came to a crashing halt on April 20th, 1987, at the age of only 25. A semi driver with diabetes went into a diabetic coma while driving his eighteen wheeler. That semi, the 80,000 pound bullet, barreled towards the bridge and stole my father's precious life.

The weird thing is that I remember every single detail of the day he died. My memory is perfect up until my shattered mother delivered the news to me. My next memory sets the foundation for this book.

The day my father was laid to rest, both of my mothers, my step father, and all of my grandparents sat on the front row of the little church on the outskirts of our population 4,444 town. My memory begins when I was sitting on my mother's lap. I remember seeing the flag, the one that veterans earn, draped across his casket. I could clearly see the abundance of flowers that stretched from wall to wall across the front of the church. Due to the horrific end to my father's life, it had to be a closed casket ceremony. His picture had been framed and placed perfectly in the middle of it all.

I can only describe the feeling as well as my broken, young mind could describe or even interpret it. I was destroyed and crying uncontrollably, barely able to see the blurry casket holding the man that used to hold me. My mom later told me that I cried for months. I couldn't stop, and I didn't care if I did. On that day, I was sitting on my mother's lap. She needed to stand up, so I was passed to the lap of the next family member, then the next, and the next. I remember each person hugging me and telling me that it was going to be okay. There was one person who said something different, and when he spoke, I believed him: "I've got you lad. I will take care of you. You're my boy." I still remember the pain in his words; they seared my soul in that moment. My grandpa spoke with such strength that I knew he meant what he said. Even today, it is the single longest-held promise anyone has ever made to me.

Grandpa's Nuggets

Beyond the day of the funeral, everything else is pretty much a blur. For a large section of my childhood, several months, I don't remember anything at all, not a single memory. Somewhere in that three or four months, my grandpa got in the habit of spending time with me. He would come and pick me up on Friday afternoons when school let out. I would go stay with grandpa just about every Friday to Sunday night when he would take me home and leave me in the care of my mom. During the summers, I would spend large chunks of my summer with grandpa. Life with grandpa was so refreshing.

I lived in a weird time where my mom and my stepfather were at the top of their game. They had reached what they felt was the epitome of success. Together they made $40,000 or $50,000 a year. Our families combined, and we had five kids living in the house. All of the kids had some kind of food in their belly. There was food in the fridge. My parents could afford television, cigarettes, beer, and whatever else that they felt created a good life.

The problem that I noticed in our home was detrimental. The same thing happened daily. With five kids at home, my mom and stepfather had to work. They went to work just to get off work. They would come home, fix something to eat together, and then sit in the living room in front of the TV the rest of the night. At bedtime they took their meager existence to bed to sleep. They got up at 4:00 AM and headed to work. Every day it was the same thing. They were back by 4:00 PM, right in front of the TV, with food on a TV tray by 5:30. That is where they spent the next five hours of every single night. My mom and stepfather thought they had a great life.

The downside to living this way is that your children don't form a connection with the adults. There was no family unit. Children miss out on the conversational aspect of relationship building between the family, as parents and children and as siblings. It deflates and defeats so many objectives as parents that we have for our children. The ability for them to communicate, the ability for them to rationalize, as well as the ability to hear the decision-making process out loud. It defeats their ability to form close and lasting bonds with people. It makes them very shallow and often children will only learn how to live right in the immediate now.

Why am I so confident about family interaction? It's simple. By grandpa grabbing me every Friday night and dropping me off every Sunday night, I saw a whole new world. For two days out of every week, I got to stay in a home without TV or without any technology. At grandpa's house we worked together as a family, and we ate together as a family. Best of all, I was communicated with as a person and not just a kid. At grandpa's house no one said, "Hey. Go to your room." or "Get out from under my feet." I was more likely to hear, "I'm going to go work. Get your boots. Come with me."

You see, grandpa had a hog farm, worked a full-time job, and mowed. Professionally mowed. He would mow cemeteries and commercial properties. A business that my father and my uncle Jim had started when they were just boys. To this day, and I'm almost 40, so over 30 years later, my uncle still mows those different properties. My uncle still works at the same place that my grandfather worked. My uncle still runs another business that my grandfather had started, that upon my grandfather passing away, my uncle stepped in and restarted. You see in that aspect of myself, my uncles, and even some of my cousins, my grandfather left an incredible legacy.

I will be forever grateful for the times that I spent with my grandpa. He taught me so many lessons. Grandpa would drop an abundance of wisdom on me every time I was with him in the day to day activities. I was completely starved all week, longing for those conversations. When he said something to me, I took it to heart. I believed him. He had never let me down. He had given me advice and pointed me in the right direction countless times. Every time he gave me a little nugget, he would look me dead in the eyes and ask me the exact same question, "You savvy lad?" Are you savvy lad? Do you understand me? Did that sink in? My entire childhood, I couldn't get through a conversation without grandpa hitting me with the, "Savvy lad?" The best part about him asking me is that it has made me at the end of every conversation think, "Wait. Do I truly understand?"

Now when I was younger grandpa definitely thought I was a little bit of a nitwit. He certainly didn't imagine that I was absorbing as much knowledge as I was. However, I was so starved for intelligent conversation, I was soaking up all of his advice. I couldn't get an adult in my life to talk to me like an adult. That was, until I was around my grandmother and grandfather. Therefore, I wanted every nugget he had.

There are a million of grandpa's nuggets that I have learned. I'll sprinkle them throughout this book. I am just hoping that somewhere in this, you will get something that is truly inspirational to you. More importantly, at the end of every one of these lessons, just ask yourself, "Savvy? Do I understand what was just said? Can I uptake the lesson that was just dropped on me?". If not, spend some time, go back, listen to it again, read it again, do whatever you're doing until you fully understand the concepts.

My grandpa didn't realize the impact he was making at the time. From the time I was seven years old until I was 25 years old, grandpa dropped nuggets on me every time I was around him. He thought he was just trying to keep me out of trouble and pointing me towards getting a good job. What he was actually doing was building a mindset of a millionaire. He gave me the exact nuggets that I needed to go out into the world, and as long as I applied them, I could crush it. He was savvy enough to understand the principles, and he was bold enough to do most of them. With the exception of just a couple of areas in his life, you see, he was taught to play it safe. He was taught to get the retirement, build the nest egg, stay on that safe side of the line.

Early on in my life, from seven years old, I realized you can lose absolutely everything that matters in a moment. Therefore in my lifetime, that shift, those two little clicks on the dial that I needed were given to me when I was just seven years old. I accumulated all that savvy wisdom from grandpa and was built into a shrewd entrepreneur. I am somebody who recognizes these lessons that I'm going to show you and share with you. You can duplicate these nuggets as it's an extremely practical and easily followed path. I don't believe that many of these guys who are running around currently promoting themselves as marketing geniuses truly understand what it means. Why do I say that? Because I listen to their words, and frankly, I watch their actions. I watch how they live, and they just don't seem very darn savvy.

I Wanna Be Rich

For as long as I can remember when somebody would ask me what am I going to do for a living, I knew the exact answer. When someone wanted to know what did I want to be when I grow up, I knew that too. I want to be rich. I have always wanted to be rich. My response was, "I'm going to be a millionaire. I'm going to be able to buy whatever I want and travel wherever I want to go. I'm going to be able to experience anything I want because I'm going to be rich. I want to be rich like those guys on TV." Those were my thoughts about adulthood for as long as I can remember.

My family would often watch television shows, in my very modest home where I was raised, for entertainment. My five brothers and sisters would gather around the television for our daily dose of fun. Many times an actor or actress would fly across the television screen in a sports car like a Ferrari, a Maserati, or a Lamborghini. I would always point and say, "I'm going to have one of those. I'm going to be rich." I didn't know the path to create wealth at the time. I just knew in my core that I was going to someday stand among the elite on the podium, in the winner's circle, waving the checkered flag because I had won the game. Winning the game to me meant to own the best car, fly to the coolest places, and have everything that made me happy.

An Outsider

I knew in my heart, in my core, that at some point I would be rich. For me there was no other choice. If I could take any one of you and put you in the circumstances that I was standing in when I was proclaiming this over my life, not a single person reading this would ever think that my richest dreams would become my reality. No one could have peered into my world as a child and thought great things would come from me. My world was chaos. It would have been tough to find someone that truly believed in me, other than my grandpa.

You see, my mother rode an emotional roller coaster nearly my entire childhood. She struggled immensely dealing with all sorts of different kinds of addictions and abuses. She was trying to survive in a house full of kids. Our house was full of my stepfather's children, the ones that he had prior to marrying my mother, and then the two that he had with her. My mom had her own nightmares from her childhood and losing my dad sent her into a whirlwind of highs and lows.

Growing up with a blended family was an endless battle. I was the black sheep. I was the only kid in the house who wasn't my stepfather's biological child. As a young person, I often felt like I didn't fit in anywhere. Even though it was painful, it was really a gift. This gift allowed me early on in life to get *comfortable* being an outsider. This is something that you will have to be content with if you are truly going to pursue this path of entrepreneurship. To pursue a path of life that is different from your surroundings is uncomfortable for most people. However, my entire life I have been pursuing exactly what everyone else has told me is impossible. That feeling of discomfort is not an obstacle that stops my progression.

Against All Odds

My grandfather never once objected to my conversations about being rich. He only said to me, "Lad", grandpa often referred to me as lad despite not having any Irish ancestry at all, "if you always spend so much time looking at the top rung of the ladder, you will never see the one right in front of your face." I have never been one to not speak to the things that I felt the most passionate about. Grinning I looked up into his eyes and said, "I am not just staring like everyone else. I'm jumping up and trying to grab the top rung. If I miss the top, I will still be several steps ahead of everyone else!" He simply smiled and lifted his brows as high as he could. In retrospect one of the greatest things he ever did for me was something that he actually didn't do. Grandpa *never* spoke negativity over my life! He simply did his best to guide my trajectory.

Back in my home my mother and her husband had pinnacled in their own minds. Between them they were making $40,000 to $60,000 a year. They could come home and eat steak at night a couple of times a week. While the kids, most of the time, would get a version of dinner. It seems like we grew up eating hot dogs and macaroni and cheese. The kids in my family would be put at the table to eat. Meanwhile the parents would sit in the living room with their dinner served on TV trays. That way they could enjoy dinner and watch their favorite television program in peace. My parents had a children are to be seen and not really heard mentality. The kids in my family were left to our own vices, left to our own imaginations, left to our own voices, and left to each other to figure out how to do life. It felt like we were more of a burden to our parents than a blessing. We were given no faith, church, or mentors that I recognized at the time.

Due to my childhood environment, I would spend countless hours playing alone. Spending the days alone gave me plenty of time to use my imagination. About ten minutes walking distance from our house was an old abandoned railroad track spur. The city had long ago removed the railroad track and had created a perfect elevated path with trees on both sides. This was an ideal place for any young man to explore. I would head down the tracks imagining and conversing with multitudes of characters that I had created in my own head. I felt a little crazy. I didn't know if it was normal or not, but I was able to create the most elaborate tales. Most always ending in my successful triumph over villains and self created struggles. I would not only defeat the bad guys, I would also get the girl and somehow manage to parlay into millions of dollars! The perfect storybook ending every single time. I would allow myself to be so engrossed that I would forget reality. My realness was that I was a poor little kid from Brookfield, Missouri. Even as reality sunk back in as I approached my home, sun setting or sometimes having already set, I would remember I wasn't a hero. I rarely got a nod from the girls, and I didn't have any money. Although I knew of those three things to be true right now. I also knew the one thing that would absolutely happen in my future was, I would be rich. I would not be poor my whole life. I could feel it!

When someone would ask what are you going to be when you grow up, I would look them dead in the eyes and as serious as I could be, give the same answer every single time. I would tell them, "I am going to be rich." Most people would challenge me by saying things like, "Oh, yeah? Of course you will get rich!" Many of those sophisticated adults would walk away rolling their eyes as they blew me off as a dumb kid. A funny little side note, at least three of the people that I remember chastising me as a child have at some point either tried to borrow *my* money or asked me for large personal cash gifts.

I imagine that someone who's reading this right now has that fiber, that tinge, that pull, that you're supposed to be more than what you are today. My thought for you is that you have the ability to accomplish whatever you want. You need a couple of things to succeed. I'm going to map out the formula in this book to enrich your life, to help you succeed, to help you become greater than who you are today.

Becoming Greater

I promise, if you go through life externally speaking, "I'm going to be rich," without understanding why you want the riches, then there will be a tough journey ahead. You have to understand why the pull is so powerful. Even if you have a good idea of your motivation, this is going to be a hard row to hoe without the right people speaking into your life. Pursuing greatness is a lifestyle that is not going to be easy. What you are reading is not a fluff book or an assortment of conceptual hoohaws. I have suggestions for your life that will alter *your* course. My recommendations will truly, genuinely work over and over again to push you past the plateau, ensuring your success.

You've probably already read the cover, but just in case you haven't, I've successfully started and exited a dozen companies to date. The idea of growing a business is fascinating to me! My team is currently running a case study company in the automotive industry, because I feel like that industry is broken. I believe that once we are embedded into the industry, my team will be able to look for disrupting opportunities and scale.

In the last decade alone, I am single-handedly responsible for between 200 and 250 million dollars in retail sales in North America and Canada. How did this happen when as a child I was told multiple times that I didn't even have a chance?

Choosing to become greater than the circumstances that could be seen in my life was my only option. I joke with people and tell them that you could have sat in my living room and felt the wind blow. If it blew hard enough outside, you could have seen my hair blowing in the wind inside of our home. It wasn't quite that bad, but it wasn't far from it. Being raised in this environment gave me the springboard into my future, but it required work, preparation, planning, and taking risks.

I once heard my stepfather say to my older brother, "We are what you would consider upper-middle class." Five kids, $60,000 a year in income, up to his eyeballs in debt, living in a household with addiction, abuse, and all the other kinds of nonsense imaginable doesn't sound like upper-middle class to me. Looking back, my circumstances were unsurmountable for many. You may have been raised in a similar environment, or maybe your childhood consisted of picket fences and rosebushes. Either way, you deserve to learn from my upbringing. This book is to help you regardless of your foundation, regardless of where you started, regardless of what you've been through, and regardless of where you stand today. This book is designed and written with one goal in mind: to show you that wealth is extremely possible and easily duplicatable if you're willing to do the work. Your future is in your hands. Take my knowledge, and grow into your greatness.

You can't build on the concepts and guesses of men.
You have to start with a solid:

FOUNDATION

If you can't create a strong mental foundation,
the things you attempt to build will crash around you.

Turning A Corner

It was the beginning of 2016, and it had been about six months since I had sold my last company. A 220 seat smokehouse, a restaurant, bar and grill, very high-end, very beautiful, very... just a great little business. This restaurant was the final business in my portfolio. You see, 24 months prior to closing on that property and that business, I had six functioning companies at one time. Unfortunately, I had lost my passion for nearly every one of them. I found myself getting into businesses because I could. I thought they were quality companies because I thought they would make good money. It was in **_2015_** that, unbeknownst to me, I had lost my entrepreneurial passion.

In the beginning of November 2015, I sold the final company, the Brickhouse Bar & Grill. Within the six month time period after selling my restaurant, I thought, "I have enough passive income, commercial real estate, apartment buildings, a stake in a small trucking company owned by my father-in-law, that I could just retire." There would be enough income to pay my bills indefinitely with just a little bit of maintenance. The properties would increase in value and I would wait. As additional properties became available I would snatch those up as well. I would continue to build this little nest egg of properties that would eventually create a great foundation. These properties would just continue to build equated wealth in myself, my family, and my companies. However, in respect to all operational distribution, product, and retail companies, I made a conscious decision to exit them all.

At this point I had just a little bit of maintenance and nothing but time on my hands, so I was in the very best shape of my life physically. Nonetheless, I was bored. I was so bored in fact, I toyed with an idea that I knew was a gimmick. There were these people running around offering me an opportunity. The pretend-to-be-in-business song and dance, known as multi-level marketing, that offered quick money. By the way I just worded that, you can probably tell that I don't necessarily believe in this model. I think it's really great and serves a role in the marketplace, but it is not for me. I will chat more specifically later in the book specifically on MLMs, or multi-level marketing. For the sake of this story, I can just tell you that two school teachers were crushing a multi-level marketing company in my little community of 5000 people.

This dynamic duo were in a company called Nerium. A face cream was the primary product they sold at the time I decided to join. I made the decision to join this company and sprint. I wanted to see what I could accomplish. Now several months prior, right when I sold the Brickhouse, I bought myself a position in this company but didn't do anything. I told the two teachers I would pay for the membership if they would just leave me alone. I thought they would get some commission and stop bothering me. At that point, I had no plans of being an active member of a multilevel marketing company. I paid for the membership in November. By March, I was bored and thought, "What the hell? Let's just see what happens."

So for the next 40 days, I sprinted at this MLM. I built an organization of about 380 people. I qualified for commissions right at $20,000. I was featured as the top recruiting agent inside of the company. A little blurb in their version of Success Magazine said, "Number one, Michael and Joy Munsterman!" Because of this, I flew out to an event hosted by Nerium, and they introduced me to all the top performers. I met people who had been in the company for a really long time. They introduced me to the rollers and the wheels of the brand. I had crowds of people gathering around me to hear what caused my success, and it was simple. I was just working my tail off.

I was cordially invited to sit in the front few rows amongst the crowd of all of these people who were jacked. I hadn't entirely earned my spot there yet, but I was on route to in the next 90 days. I looked behind me at everybody else in attendance, and I saw a sea of people who wanted it so badly but didn't know how to actually get it. I immediately felt hollow. In the 24 months prior to that moment, I had exited a company that did $48 million in gross sales in its best year. I had just under 400 employees from coast to coast, with manufacturing in Vietnam, in Taiwan, and in mainland China. I was importing products and distributing them through fortune 500 companies like Tractor Supply Company and Ace Hardware. I had been negotiating deals with companies like Lowe's America and getting product placement in Lowe's Canada. I had been negotiating with Canadian Tire company and many others. I had went from this incredible business to sitting three rows deep from the stage at a multilevel marketing event with a bunch of hype and hoorah. I was surrounded by people who wanted to taste real business but didn't know the path. I was empty.

I faked it; no one around me knew. Only one person could see the dead space in my eyes, and that was my wife. So I got back home from the event, and I made a decision. I'm not going to do anything in this company for 30 days, and I want to see what happens. When I left for this convention there were 392 active people in my downline, people who wanted to sprint, wanted to be successful, wanted to have a business, and wanted to drive and hustle. Only a couple of those 392 are still in the company from the last I heard. The teachers who recruited me made some excuses about the company and left. Now they are onto another MLM company, and they continue to blast the internet with why they love relationship marketing.

The truth is, if those same people would invest in themselves and if they'd experienced what I experienced, they would realize that they're eating tasteless food. It will never be their legacy. It will never be their story. It will never be their results. It will always just be somebody else's company, and they will forever, in one capacity or another, still be working for a higher boss, as long as they continue down the path of multilevel marketing. This perfect machine is designed for people who want to be in business for themselves. It is created for the few elite who can actually operate at scale and capacity; those few can go in and make a ton of money. However, they have to look in the mirror every day and know they are faking value through over-hyped products that require an 800% markup. **Side-note: 800% markup is the number that was given to my by the founder of HERBALIFE, a well known nutrition company that seen its heyday in the early to mid 2000's before going public. That means every product you purchase through MLM has been marked up 800%. Compare that to a space heater you would purchase at your local hardware store that has around a 25-40% markup.**

MLM want-repreneurs stare in the mirror and recognize they are taking advantage of people that just want a better life. They look across the table from people and say, "You can do this." MLMs know entirely well that the eager, yet ignorant people, cannot actually make any money. Please don't get me wrong, I don't even want to call them ignorant. They're good people, they just don't realize they don't have the capacity to succeed in an MLM. Knowing what it takes to build to that level, the MLM representative is looking across the table at a lady who's going to give them a large percentage of her nest egg, knowing that she can't perform, knowing she'll never reach what she hopes she can reach. The innocent victim is sitting there hoping she can create additional income for her life.

My wife saw that dead space in my eyes. She saw in my eyes that there was no way that this was long-term for me. She knew that I needed to remind myself that I was designed to hunt. I need to know that I was designed to scale, that I was designed to lead, that I was designed to coach, to teach, and to mentor. She could clearly see that I was dying on the vine.

An Unexpected Video

One Saturday morning I woke up with no reason to get up. Typically, when I'm actively pursuing a venture, I'm a 5:00 A.M. guy. I'll talk more about that in a future chapter. However, when you don't have any hustle, anything to grind, anything to scale, anything to pursue, there's no reason to get out of bed before 7:00 A.M. On that particular morning I realized my wife had stayed up late Friday night on her phone. I wasn't sure what she was up to and I fell asleep. When I woke up, it was twenty minutes before seven. Out of habit, I looked at my phone, that's what most of us do, the very first thing we roll out of bed, we look at our phones. Some of us use the bright light of our phone to jumpstart our brain. I'm definitely guilty of that.

I looked at my phone and I had a message from my wife, a Facebook message. I clicked on messenger and I went into the app. I clicked on her name and it was a link to a video. I thought, "Well she's laying in bed asleep, I want to see what this video is." It was Wake Up Warrior, the have it all lifestyle. I thought "interesting." Immediately, I go in the other room to get more information. I click on the link and it's an hour-long video of a guy by the name of Garrett J. White. He is standing on a bridge in Las Vegas ranting about how more than likely I was a one-dimensional douchebag. He was calling me and every other married businessman that might have stumbled onto this video a pussy. It intrigued me. I thought, "This guy, he's standing on a bridge and he's screaming at me telling me that I am broken.'"

It clicked, "Why would my wife send this video to me?" There was tons of profanity in it. My wife is not interested in profanity. She's not into profanity at all. It's not her bag, and this guy's dropping F-bombs, boom, boom, boom, boom, boom. Then it dawned on me, "She knows that I'm sad. She knows that currently in my life I'm a caged lion who is unable to hunt and unable to perform at my full capacity. My food is being brought to me every day. It's being dropped at my feet." Money was rolling in. We had long forgotten the days of want or need, or worrying about, "Will we ever run out of money?" We had gotten to a point where income was just coming. It was literally *income*-ing. It was everything I thought that I needed and it was happening. Unfortunately, I was dead inside, and she knew it.

At the end of this video, this guy says, "Apply below to secure your spot in Warrior Week." I could not resist. I had to learn more. It just so happened that I ended up being in Warrior Week 28. I flew out to the beaches of Laguna for the week. I went through what Garrett affectionately refers to as the crucible; five days of being fully submerged in an experience that was designed to break you. Then with you broken, he shows you some insights and some realities. Not insights and realities to the outside world but insights and realities to your world, to your heart, to what you want, who you are, who you're designed to be, but mostly who it's okay for you to be. It was a lesson that I needed. He was the mentor that I needed.

Becoming a Warrior

That process, that week, that ticket, that crazy expensive experience changed me. Inside of the seven days traveling to and back from Warrior I spent more than most people make in a year. I did that so that I could run with a group of men that were as powerful or more powerful than myself. I have a place where I could speak openly about successes, wins, failures, and not worry about being judged. This week provided to me an outlet where I can converse without worrying about somebody coming at me or without worrying about somebody having professional jealousy. Having a group to listen without worrying about somebody giving me advice because they were biased and their opinion actually had weight in an area. Warrior gave me a group of true entrepreneurs to have fellowship that was not a relative, not a family member, not a wife, not a kid, not a brother, not a sibling, not just a warm body. These were just men who were in the same sprint searching for the same thing I was; permission to hunt.

When I stepped onto the beaches of Laguna for the first day, we had been given very specific instructions on the gear that we needed to bring. Combat boots, BDUs, t-shirts that were logo'd specifically for the event. Black head to toe. We were brought out, no watches, nothing weird on your wrists. No rings allowed.

Our thought was very much we were getting ready to do a workout, but we weren't dressed like we were gonna work out. Combat boots and BDUs typically not workout attire for civilians. They rushed us out into a line where they made us recite Invictus.

> Out of the night that covers me,
> Black as the pit from pole to pole,
> I thank whatever gods may be
> For my unconquerable soul.
>
> In the fell clutch of circumstance
> I have not winced nor cried aloud.
> Under the bludgeoning of chance
> My head is bloody, but unbowed.
>
> Beyond this place of wrath and tears
> Looms but the Horror of the shade,
> And yet the menace of the years
> Finds, and shall find me, unafraid.
>
> It matters not how strait the gate,
> How charged with punishments the scroll,
> I am the master of my fate:
> I am the captain of my soul.

We had to recite it quickly. There were guys yelling at us. We couldn't misstep. Then we were blindfolded and taken by van to a grinder mat. If you don't know what a grinder mat is, a grinder mat's essentially just a great big hard surface. They had put some rubber workout material down that could get wet, and they started football drilling us. "Run in place. Drop to the ground. Do push ups. Jump up. Do a burpee. Jump up. Get on your back. Get on your feet. Do more pushups. Do some sit ups. Do more pushups. Plank. Do bear squats. Go." On and on this went. Next we heard the fire hose come on, or some kind of a high pressure hose that started to spray us. We are in what I would consider non-water-wearing attire getting sprayed with water. Boots are getting wet. Faces getting wet. Clothes, pants, underwear, socks, everything getting very, very wet, and we're just continuously grinding and grinding and grinding on the grinder.

Finally I hear, because we're still blindfolded, I hear some of the coaches coming and grabbing different people. I could hear them taking people away and bringing them back. Continuously taking them away and bringing them back, taking them away and bringing them back. At this point, I had no idea where they were going. In fact, I thought that they had forgot about me. Suddenly I felt a hand grab my arm. The guy literally said to me, "You didn't think we forgot you, did you? Follow me." He guided me not very far, about 25 or 30 paces from where I was standing. I could still hear the guys working out in the background.

Why?

Revelations of an Ice Bath

This voice says to me, "Why are you here?" This answer was simple. I was broken. I knew that I needed a new hustle. I needed a new venture, and I wanted to figure out what industry was next. I simply said, "I'm here for business." He said, "Very good. Raise your left foot, and step forward for me. Be careful." I raised my left foot, and I stepped forward. "Go ahead and put your foot down." I set my foot down, and it went into an ice bath. It went into a freaking ice bath, knee deep and it was freezing. I thought, "Holy shit, this is cold."

"Why are you here?" came the voice screaming! "I'm here because I want to figure out what my next business is," I replied. The voice came at me again, "Raise your right foot for me. Go ahead and step forward. Both feet in." Now I'm up to my knees in ice water. The voice asked again, "Why-are-you-here?" I had the same response, "I'm here to figure out how I want to continue to scale and make money." Apparently the voice did not like my answer as I heard, "Go ahead and have a seat."

This time, they have me sit all the way up to my neck in a freezing cold tub of ice. Now I'm cold. This isn't cold water. This is an ice bath. If you've never done this, you need to do this. Sitting in an ice bath is a skill that will follow you, and it will strengthen you. It's the entire purpose that I'm telling you this continuous story. I'm up to my neck in ice water. I am slightly physically exhausted, but capable of doing the workout. I am extremely cold. It is that first 60 to 90 seconds of being in ice water, what you might or might not realize is, that it hurts before it numbs. And I was in the pain stage. I was physically exhausted, and now cold prickly needles all over my skin. "Why are you here?" came the voice. I continuously gave the same shallow answer over and over. Only this last time they started to pour ice water directly on the crown of my head.

Now I'm just miserable. I feel like I'm slipping in and out of consciousness. I feel like my eyes are squinting closed to keep the cold water from making my eyeballs hurt anymore. I can feel the ice chips hitting the top of my head, and through the water, through the pain, through everything I hear it again, "Why are you here?"

I just broke down. The misery was unsurmountable. I answered by screeming, "I don't know what you expect me to say!" They lifted my blindfold to an iPad opened up to Facebook with a picture of my family. In that moment, in that second, I began to cry, and I uttered the words, "I'm here for them." Finally, they stood me up. I started to crumple back down just a little bit, and they grabbed me to stop me from falling. Looking into the eyes of my Warrior coach the voice, his voice, said, "That is your why."

I share this with you, not because my why is relevant to you, but because that's what I had to go through to see what my why truly was. I had to remove layers of lies and stories. I had to get beyond being physically exhausted. I had to shock my body through pain. I had to be suffering to realize the raw answer to this question: What is my why? Why do I hustle? Why do I grind? Why do I put in 18-hour days? Why am I relentless? Why wasn't I willing to quit? When things got tough, why do I persevere? When companies all around me were failing in the '08 crisis, why did my company scale from my living room to 50 million dollars a year in sales? It was the girls in my family, my wife and my daughters. They are my why. They are the reason.

Now I've done some work since then, and I recognize that I have lots of layers to my specific why. My initial why, my sprint away from poverty, and being 300 thousand dollars in debt in 2005, and my why for being a multimillionaire by 2010 was different. My why in those periods was to escape poverty and to change my family's story. However, I realized that a person can only earn so much money. You can only own so many cars. You can only buy a certain caliber of house before it exceeds the need of your family. There's a point where you get on your phone and think, "I want to buy something, but I have everything I want." Literally you will spend $500, $600, $800, or $1000 just because you can. If you are like me, you will buy the dumbest things. Then you'll find out that those material items are nothing. They mean nothing. They bring nothing. They won't make you happier. They won't make you feel more fulfilled. They won't lift you up. They won't feed the lion. Savvy?

As men and women who are wired to hunt, or to pursue excellence, we are driven differently than the rest of the world. Few people are wired for this hunt; few are motivated to pursue growth and expansion to create the success they've envisioned. We have to be driven by a why that genuinely matters. Our why must be our passion. It must be so tied to our being that when we talk about it, emotions rise in our bodies. When I'm talking about these integral moments, like the moment that blindfold was lifted, I have to fight back tears. When I talk about my family, my past, and my history, I feel the wave of my emotions begin to overpower the dam I've built to conceal them.

I don't cry all the time. In any circle you would place me, I would be considered a guy's guy. I love guns and to hunt. I love to work out. I love to build things with my hands. I'm not the kind of guy that tears up very easily—until you get close to my why. That's when you know you've grasped onto something that has true relevance. I've heard people reference things they care about. I've heard people explain their why, and it's different than any other blasé conversation. If you're going to succeed and if this book is going to do you any good at all, then you need to associate so tightly with your why. Anytime you feel safe enough to share that vulnerability with someone, they shouldn't hear your words, but they should feel your heart. When they look deep in the eyes of the lion, they see a hunter. Savvy?

Climbing Your Mountain

Social media today has altered the way that John Q. Public perceives entrepreneurship. There are images of cars, trips, lifestyles, and clothes; everything looks easy and fun. It seems as though anybody can start a business, call themselves an entrepreneur, crush it, get rich, and win. This perception directly ties to the reason I'm spending so much time telling you my story of finding my why.

It took me a lifetime of poverty, insecurities, frustrations, and people telling me that I would never make it. I had a life of failures, missteps, and mess ups. It took a lifetime of tragedy, mourning, and sadness to prepare me. I'm not saying that everything was terrible. I'm just saying that those mountains are in the journey. Some of the obstacles are just little hills that are pretty easily climbed over, and life is good. Some of these obstacles are enormous, like Mount Everest is in your path. These struggles often seem insurmountable. Here's what will happen to the average person. Time will grab them by the collar and drag them through life, and they'll close their eyes and shut out the journey. The average guy will hit a mountain like Mount Kilimanjaro and time will just pull him around the base of the same mountain. Like a continuous cycle, he will struggle with his mountain over and over again in his head. Most people will be trapped in the same circle around the bottom of their own Mount Everest.

You see, time doesn't owe anyone any favors. Time is just time. Time is just there. It's real; it's a law. You're hoping that in time you'll get so familiar with the base of your mountain that you'll learn how to navigate it best. Entrepreneurs understand they're on a journey that's bigger than one mountain or one story. Emotionally successful people will not allow their path to wrap around the base of a mountain because of a single story. These few, recognize that mountains are just roadblocks before the true greatness that is held farther down on their path. Now I'm not saying that entrepreneurs are impervious to struggles. If I spend an hour in a business that is just big enough for one self-employed person and I visit with the owner for just a short while, I can determine why their business cannot get off the ground. I can tell you the story, or the mountain, that time has been dragging them around. I can tell you what's holding them back and keeping them in the same circling pattern, sometimes for decades.

The only way to truly track down this path and overcome the small hills and Everests in your life is to truly understand the destination. This is where the analogy gets a little bit elusive because the destination is every single step you take. What do I mean by that? I mean that I recognize every single hurdle I have to overcome. Every single step I have to take while working ahead and moving against my mountain requires that I grab onto my destination, which is directly attached to my why. My destination is to provide a legacy for generations, to impact the masses, and to maybe just help one guy or girl with a similar story to me. I am always hoping to impact thousands, hoping to leave a legacy for my family, and hoping to drive ahead into something that impacts the multitudes. Every single step I take moving closer to my destination is rooted to that why. Every single step is for my family.

As I talked about earlier, when you get so deeply rooted to your why, it becomes emotional. When you choose to share that intimate why with someone, it will jerk on your heart cords. You'll need that. You will need that pull whenever you're fighting with time, fighting with a story, or fighting to overcome the obstacles that are put in your path. It's not always sexy, but when it is, it's terrific. You know, the great thing about climbing a mountain happens right before you get to ease down the other side. You get to bask in that victory, when you are standing at the top you stake your flag in it, and scream, "I conquered this!"

Getting to the top of the mountain is a fantastic feeling. You have overcome the obstacle laid before you. You get to look 360 degrees and all sides clear of the stress of the mountain. All sides are clear of the battle and clear of the weight of everything you just went through to get to the top. It is in those moments you'll find clarity. Your view is so clear and it becomes so easy to have a vision for the future. You see, once you have peaked and you have jabbed your flag which represents your success into the peak of that overwhelming mountain. In those moments of realization, the vision for moving ahead becomes so clear. The clarity of vision is there because you can look down, you can see the path you just traveled more clearly. You've just overcome one of the biggest obstacles in your life or maybe you're overcoming it right now. When you look down, it is more clear than ever. After making it to the top, you can enjoy the view from there for a moment, and after taking in the clear vision, you begin the descent.

You head back down into the trenches. You're not stopping and patting yourself on the back after each step, you are already on to the next destination. You will find yourself moving ahead with a new vigor and a new excitement. You see, whether I'm winning or whether I'm losing, I recognize that it is all just my perception. Whether you're winning or whether you're losing, your perception of that experience is what defines your journey.

If you truly wanna have a journey that is all inspiring and inspirational, if you truly wanna have a journey that every single day you spring out of bed to chase, you have to learn how to remind yourself insistently of your why. Savvy?

Remembering Your Why

One of the things that I do every single day to remind myself of my why is I take a cold shower in the morning. That's tied so directly to my ice bath when I was reintroduced to my newest layer of my why. My family, my wife, Joy, and my beautiful daughters, Brooke and Maggie, they are my mafia level why. Every morning the ice cold water pelting against my skin reminds me of the experience. That cold water reinforces the reason I am the first one up and the last one to sleep every single day! Hustling harder than anyone I know! As I write this book, I am sitting in Turks and Caicos. My family is down at the beach enjoying the water. For me getting this message out to you and hopefully impacting the masses is more important than my short term wants and desires.

I knew I cared about my family. I knew I was providing for my family, but I wasn't rooted deep enough to realize my driving force. I was still running around the same mountain of I don't wanna be poor. I listed to the stories of: I don't want my daughters to be poor, I don't want my children to have the struggles that I had, I don't want my kids to ever look under a Christmas tree and think where is everything? I don't want my daughters to worry or wonder unless they choose this lifestyle. I want it to be their decision, their journey, their story. If I am successful there will be a paragraph in the story of them that includes, "My dad recognized that in order for us to have the opportunity, he had to sacrifice!" Literally there are so many little stories like that that I can tell you. As a child I put a fake smile on my face to not disappoint the people around me. All the while, I myself was disappointed, and I never want my children to experience that.

There are some people who will disagree with me and think you should let your kids have some failures. Why? Why can't you give your family the best version of life? I was giving them everything which made me believe that escaping poverty was still my why. Neck deep in that ice water looking into that iPad, staring ahead at the picture of my family, it hit me like a ton of bricks. I've scaled that mountain, and I was just flooded with emotion. Tears instantly began pouring down my checks as they stood me up and pulled me out of the ice. It hit me. I don't have to run from that anymore. I can stand on the top and look around. My vision was clear. I could now sprint ahead at the next goal! This is exactly what I want for you! I want you to be able to get clear on your why, look around, and then sprint into action!

Just to kind of summarize, I think it's important that you walk away from this with a couple things. This is a wonderful, rewarding journey that never has a boring day. You'll be scared. You'll be insecure. You'll have to deal with employees and budgets. You'll have doubts. You'll have naysayers. Those doubts bundled together will cause you to question whether it's worth it. However, if you are rooted deep into your why, every single time you face one of those challenges, you'll smile because you'll have already have won. Savvy?

Business in a Box

& Getting Advice From a Fortune Cookie Coach!

It's incredible! So many times in my life I've had somebody step in just for a very brief period and say, "Have you ever thought about this?" Some of those "have you thought abouts" are just absolute asinine and won't work at all. Then some of them have been gold, like just absolute gold. This is what we look for, when dealing with mentors or anyone for that matter. The dumbest person you know could potentially regurgitate the exact wisdom nugget that you have been seeking. Too many arrogant people exist in this world, people that think they don't need to take the time to listen to anyone who they don't see as being on their level or higher. Am I saying that you will get rich by lowering to your lowest influencer level? Absolutely not! I'm saying God could speak to you through anyone, if you will take the time to listen.

I actually love multi-level marketers. The reason that I do is because inside of MLM, there are an abundance of really brilliant, talented people. Then there are lots of parrots. Parrots are people who learn the things to say, regurgitate the things that they hear, and they just spit it out again and again and again and again and again. Parrots have some success and feel comfortable enough to be able to call themselves entrepreneurs. However they are simply doing what they were told. "Don't reinvent the wheel. Do exactly what we do. Say exactly what we say. Present it exactly how we present it and just go, go, go, go, go, go," say most MLM manuals. One thing that I love about Multi Level Marketing Companies is that they mine through the population seeking out the self motivated individuals. Multilevel marketing companies seem to dig up every person that has ever wanted to "be their own boss".

Having stepped into that industry for a brief time really allowed me to understand what they truly had. Most MLMs offer a low barrier to market franchise opportunity. Some really great people who believe that there is more to this life than working for someone else can be found in your neighborhood MLM. Then some there are people who just want to belong to something, they find this through the community inside of multilevel marketing. Finally, there are also some true entrepreneurs who could excel and succeed in whatever they put their mind to. That is what MLM's do. They hunt for people who are truly brilliant entrepreneurs before the individual has even discovered the truth about themselves. Giving the most immature entrepreneur a cookie cutter machine and counting on the fact that their peers are similar in nature. If you asked me to define this idustry it would be as follows:

A machine that is brilliantly constructed, medicating the members with the perfect doses of resources, incentives and motivation. While the few powerhouses absorb their immediate circle of influences. Then veining their way into their friends and family, searching for that little cut of gold or those few diamonds in the rough to repeat the process again and again. A perfectly orchestrated plague that will grow rapidly killing a lot of brilliant minds and turning them forever away from their dreams of some day owning their own business. Reinforcing the fear that business is bad and if they are going to get rich it will be via the lottery. The good news is that at some point nearly all of these "fastest growing record breaking startups" have a come to Jesus moment and are rectified through some form or another, yet again leaving thousands of would be world changers devastated in the wake.

There is one extremely powerful element to this multilevel marketing machine. It is this: MLM's are the greatest testament to the power of mentorship and coaching. Not only does the MLM industry grow and build around leaders doing just that, leading. It also curates some pretty phenomenal communicators and motivators. The multilevel marketing industry spits out coaches faster than anything I've ever seen.

These coaches fire up their iPhones getting straight to work. They create videos talking about freedom. These guys become masters at delivering a lot of witty little cliché feel good comments, right?

There is a new style of this same snake oil. Some of them call themselves coaches, some consultants, some call themselves influencers. I look at them, research their history a bit and just shake my head. I hear a lot of these new-age coaches doing the same thing. These modern coaching guys, the most successful venture that they've ever had is the venture that they're pimping right now — they're a coach.

They're a mentor because they were savvy enough to set up a Click Funnels account via Russell Brunson. They watched his videos and got educated. They read a few books like Dot-Com-Secrets, which in total fairness is an awesome book. They encourage these guys by saying, "You can read a couple three books and be an expert in any field you want." At least you can be in the top 90% because most people haven't read two or three books in any given field. Most people, since they've graduated high school, haven't read two or three books.

Coaches with no actual experience in the business world will latch onto a couple different things that they hear repeatedly, and they pull them from all different areas. Some of these ideas come from other coaches. Some of the ideas come from thought leaders. Some of the ideas come from successful entrepreneurs. Some of the ideas come straight from the Bible. They will say things like seek wise counsel or you're the average of the five closest people you surround yourself. Many coaches will tell you to write your goals. A coach might even ask you what's your why? They crazy part is everything they are saying is true! These are all principles of wealth. Some of them we will talk about later in the book and they are real. Many of these principles will work. However, if you ask any one of the so called "experts" to elaborate, they would reveal their true aptitude quickly.

Grandpa would tell me, "You can't believe everything somebody tells you. You need to be a little bit level headed if you are going to figure out who you can trust and who you need to give the boot." Savvy?

Eagles or Turkeys

Over the last few years I have watched an emergence of what I call "Social Snake Oil Salesmen" build out elaborate sites that would almost fool even a seasoned entrepreneur / investor. This is was a huge incentive for me to speak up, call their bluffs and create a true roadmap to the most useful techniques you will ever find with a detailed explanation of why. The first of which is one of the principles that I think is extremely important. It's directly associated to your why. It's directly associated to the walk. It's directly associated to the path. It's directly associated to your success, it is to seek wise counsel.

Grandpa would say, "You can't soar with the eagles if you hang with a bunch of turkeys! Savvy lad?" I am sure you know exactly what he means by this. If you want to be at the top of your game, if you want the successful business, then you must form relationships with others that are successful in that area. The 'turkeys' in your life will only halt your progress. Those 'turkeys' will alter your thoughts. So as grandpa advised, please find some eagles and soar with them.

Now, I think that a lot of people do something that's a huge mistake. They call seeking wise counsel, running their mouth about their personal problems. Many people run all over the place, and they ask absolutely anybody that will listen for advice. They go through this great, big, long spiel to anybody who will listen. They're relentless, and frankly they're making a huge mistake because they're forgetting one word. They're seeking counsel but they're using counsel as a billboard to tell their business. Just to compound and throw a bunch of these sweet little nuggets that you've heard before, but then to tie it all together and make it make sense. It is seek *WISE* counsel. Seek wise counsel, and do it without loose lips. You have to strategically pick the people that you will look to for advice. They need to be accelerated beyond you in that particular area of your life where you need growth.

Tai Lopez talks about the upper 33%, the 33% of people that consist of your friends and the 33% of the people around you who you can mentor and help. His theory is you should surround yourself with the 33% a third of the time. Basically that the struggling 33% of the people in your life, you are the influencer for them. You have an obligation to lift those people higher. The 33% that are on your level, those are your peers. Those are your friends. The upper 33%, those are your mentors. Just using his belief system for the balance of this example, if you're asking questions of the lower 33%, you're bragging. If you are challenging the people around you with your ideas, your peer group, if you're taking these ideas and seeking counsel from your peers, you're not necessarily bragging, but you're definitely billboarding. You're putting your business out there to a group of people that see you as competition in life. This is a very real, very harsh reality. Some people that could see you as competition include, friends, business associates, business partners, co-workers, sorority sisters, frat brothers, cousins, neighbors, even educators.

Get ready the next few examples are hard to accept: parents, girlfriends, boyfriends, even your spouse! I know what your thinking, "Wait a second Michael! You think my wife is jealous of me?" Not necessarily. What I am saying is that this list of people, although could potentially be a great resource for wisdom in your life, unless you can 100% know for sure that their motives are strong and pure, you should filter every nugget they hand you. Filter their advice with this question: **How, positively or negatively, could this persons input be jaded or weighted based on their connection with me and their current position in life in comparison to mine?** The reality is that you can extract millions of brilliant nuggets from these people. Everything has to be filtered through the, what is their true underlying motivation behind this advice? What personal doctrines and belief systems do they have that could alter or skew this advice?

Even when you're thinking about the above questions in relation to getting advice from your peers, you have to weigh out in your mind, is this advice non biased and the very best thing for me to consider? You could also ask it like this, other than my ultimate success, what connections or belief systems does this person have that could skew their loving advice and perspective in relation to my success?

Another one that I love is, we've all heard it, loose lips sink ships. It's true. In the Godfather movies, the don, one of the things that he says is, "A strong position your thoughts can be." That's true. When you tell people your business, you give up your position. When you talk about your business, your strategies, and your moves you're giving up your position. You're telling people where you are, where you're going, and your peers are racing against you in their own minds. By racing against you in their own minds, what exactly does that mean? That means that when you're talking to them, you're telling them your business, and you're seeking their counsel, their input back to you is biased. I have a really great analogy that I'll share here in the next chapter, but first I'm going to finish this thought.

When you go to the upper 33%, when you go to your mentors, they don't see you as a dog in the race. They don't see you as somebody who is hunting their heels. Most of these guys think of you as that 33% that they want to work with and lift up, that they want want to help, that they want to encourage. You're in the 33% that if you choose to, you have somebody sticking their hand back and saying, "Here, catch up with me." They've seen it a 100 times. They have actually been in your shoes. These mentors will put that hand back there 100 times and out of 100 times maybe only had one guy grab it and pull themselves forward. Most people misunderstand the thought process of seek wise counsel. Seek wise counsel simply means this, reach forward and grab the hand. Unfortunately, what most people interpret seeking counsel as grab the hands of those around you. Savvy?

Good Mentors

And The Crabby Truth

Now I want to tell you an interesting factual story. While you are reading this story that I'm going to share with you, I want you to envision this in your mind. It will become very clear to you what it is that I'm describing, what I'm talking about. It's a super useful tool for you to decide in your conversations with those around you if they're your peers or if they're your mentors. If you're familiar with crab traps, crab traps are a really interesting thing. Crab traps, you know, a typical box like the shape of a dice has six sides. A crab trap only has five. It's completely open on the sixth side. Down in the bottom of the crab trap is a little cage that's wired to the bottom of the crab trap exactly opposite of the open side.

Can you envision this? A steel wired cage. It's about three-foot wide in both directions and four-foot tall; completely open on one side. On the bottom of the crab trap as you're looking in the open side is a little cage that's less than 10 inches square wired to the bottom of that trap. Also, when you look down, there are weights attached to the bottom of the trap. Inside of that little cage, they stuff bread crumbs or loaves or chunks of bread depending on water current, regardless, bait is stuffed into the small cage. Fishermen throw the crab trap over the edge of the boat where it sinks to the bottom of the ocean. What is interesting is that a single crab will make its way into this trap and get to the bait.

Another crab will then recognize that a fellow crab found the bait. The second crab will follow, and more, and more, and more follow to a point where lots of crabs are in this trap, now fighting to get to the bottom. All of these crabs are scrambling to get to the bread. However, long ago the bread was already consumed by the first few crabs, but people still follow. Pardon me, oops. Crabs still follow because they believe in their heart, they think that there's bait down there. You walking by as a crab, see this happening. You watch your family go into the trap. You watch your siblings go into the trap. You watch your best friends go into the trap. Everybody's telling you, "There's bait. Come on, follow us." You follow as well. You don't even think about it. Most people, probably including you, are in the trap before they ever even realize they're born into this trap, and then something incredible happens. Your eyes are opened. You realize that what everyone's fighting for doesn't exist there. If you're going to find it, you have to go in another direction. It is at that revelation that you begin to climb out of the trap.

Crabs are fascinating though, when the crabs who feel like they're working to help each other get to the bottom of the trap, see you going the other way, they grab onto you and pull you back down into the trap. In fact, crabs will completely pull apart another crab trying to escape the trap. They will kill a crab that is trying to leave the trap before they'll let it leave. Isn't that fascinating? We, as individuals in this world, we're looking around at all of the people sitting on all sides of us, and we think of them as our family, as our friends, as our peers, and they are. Their intentions for you on some level are true, loving, and from a place of a desire for you to succeed. Unfortunately, if you try to crawl out of the trap, watch what happens "for your own good."

As you're trying to climb out, you'll say, "Hey, I got this idea. There's this thing I've been thinking about. There's this book I just read. There's this concept that I just started listening to, and I really think that it's fire. I want to pursue it." Inevitably, you'll have someone speak into your life, "Look, I think you should just play it safe. I think you should just be careful. I don't know. You have a really good job. You have retirement; you have pension. You have all these good things going for you. I think you should just stay right where you are. Make the right decision." Wink, nod, and smile. You can see outside of the trap. You recognize it. There's a great big ocean and a lot more opportunity than this one little spot of bread. And you want out.

Inside of that crab trap, stop looking at yourself as as crab, and start looking at yourself as yourself standing in the middle of a bunch of crabs. Now, think in your life, who are those crabs standing around you? Who are the people that you've gone to and asked, "What about this? What about that? Could we do XYZ?" What have their responses been? Now, look up. Look to that 33% that Tai talked about, that mentor percentage, and see them standing on the edge of the trap with their hand extended down to you saying, "I believe you can get out of this." Make the decision to reach up and take their hand. Every single crab around you is going to latch onto you and try to hold you down. They will try to trap you and keep you where you're "safe." This is why you need a why. As you're seeking that wise counsel from true entrepreneurs, true businessmen, true investors, people who are standing outside of the trap themselves allow your why to focus your vision. Do not stay, hustling amongst the crabs to get out, but reach for the people that have a proven track record to succeed. Reach up and grab their hands.

This is what my information is all about. This is why I started the podcast. This is why we started mentoring and coaching people to begin with, because to my wife and I, it felt as though we came out of hiding. We just did us. We just built companies.

We just sprinted. We weren't thinking about, "I'm going to sprint and build a social media following." This is why at the time of the writing of this book, I have less than 1,000 followers on Instagram. As we push and drive ahead, I expect that to increase. People will recognize me as someone standing at the top rung of the trap sticking my hand out saying, "I'll help you if you're genuine about getting out of the trap. If you can successfully tell me your why. If your why is real and tangible, and if it is attached to your heart." If I can feel your sincerity in what you're saying to me, myself, and just a handful of other true thought leaders will gladly extend our hand to you and pull you right out of the trap. We will show you that path. We will teach you what to look for as you're climbing out. It's amazing.

The people who are stuck in the trap around you cannot see reality. The ones who were telling you, "No, no, no, no. Don't try to go against the norm!" When you get out and they think you have found your own trap, they will follow you. Instead of trying to hold you back, they will seek after you. First you must break free from the crab trap.

In essence, in the first part of this crab trap analogy, you are being able to recognize the people around you for who they are. Are they fellow crabs trying to trap you and hold you in the trap? Or are the people around you the ones standing up on the lip of the trap with their hand down trying to help you navigate safely to the vast open waters of opportunity? Or are they the people who relentlessly are digging to the bottom, the ones who will never look up? The same ones who think they are just living the hand that they have been dealt. Categorizing those people in your own mind so that you can associate them appropriately and proportionality will give you a new clear perspective to who is there to help and who maybe isn't. Savvy?

In a Box!

Elementary Mentors

The next section is about the type of mentors that you want to seek. I think that there are several different avenues that people choose to go in relation to mentors. Based on your view of success and what that might be, your view-set in that space will dictate where you can find the most effective mentors. For example, for me initially, without a lot of money and with very limited resources as far as where I lived, it was difficult to find a true mentor. I lived in a small town in north central Missouri. Born and raised in Brookfield, Missouri, population 4444. Inside of that little community, there were some successful people. However, there weren't very many successful people that would take the time to mentor a snot nosed teenage brat, like yours truly. Someone that wasn't very studious. I didn't get good grades. I wasn't a great example to my peers, I consistently got into a lot of trouble, created a lot of mischief, and barely graduated high school. Not just because I only graduated with a 1.9 GPA, but also because it seemed like regularly I was venturing down to the high school principal's office.

So, in and out of all of that, there were only a few people that chose to speak positively into my life. Few people genuinely took the time not just to talk at me, but to speak to me. Every single person reading this book can think of at least one person who has tried to help you along this journey we call life. They've given you nuggets. They've guided you based on your feedback to discover who you are and who they know you as a person to be. The potential that they see in you steers their conversations. They've spoke those positive nuggets into your life. One of the things that grandpa always said to me was, "Lad, in this world, you have to walk with your eyes open." What's so great is the absolute infinite amount of situations this statement relates. The way time works and operates for us is this, just because you weren't walking through those parts of your life thinking on that specific day, "Someday I'm gonna be rich. Someday I'm gonna be an entrepreneur." You can still look back and glean nuggets from the people who have been speaking into your world.

For me, at my fathers funeral, as I was being passed from family member to family member in an unending rotation. My grandfather latched onto me and said, "I'm going to take care of you. I will be there. I will never let you go." Basically, he was my most stable advisor until he passed away when I was 36 years old. So, for 30 years of my life, this man was one of my greatest mentors, one of my greatest teachers. He over the years was actively teaching me about life, relationships, family, and business. I didn't realize the weight of his wisdom at the time. I didn't think at the time, "Hey, this guy is teaching me how to think like a millionaire. This guy is teaching me how to think like a successful business person. This guy is teaching me how to communicate and negotiate on purpose and on fire with a focus on my objectives." You have that person too, you have those people, those family members that are stable advisors. You have educators that are trying to guide you to the next level.

When my dad died, I had a teacher in the first grade. Her name was Mrs. Moore. I'll never forget Mrs. Moore! That woman showed me so much compassion and love as a first grader as well as throughout my life. It showed me the difference that I could feel from first grade having Mrs. Moore as a teacher, to my second grade teacher that didn't recognize me for what I had been through. This second grade teacher didn't cut me any slack because of the tragedy. In her classroom she had big cardboard boxes that were designed to sit on top of a troublemaker's desk. These dividers were places to focus the troublemaker. I couldn't see the people around me and wouldn't be distracting to the class. Quite literally, I got to live in the box. Alienating me did not help my social skills. In fact, the other kids didn't understand. They just thought I did not have it all together. Maybe the other kids thought I was a little crazy from losing my dad. I am not certain their thoughts of my behavior, but I am pretty sure they weren't very positive.

I wish that from a place of integrity I could tell you that I was a good student, a hard worker, an athlete, or even a very good friend. I just wasn't any of those things. I had been shattered, I was already a bit hyper and mischievous prior to my fathers death. As I rose from the deepest depression you can ever imagine, I emerged a new little person. A rebellious almost antagonistic eight year old with zero fears. You see I couldn't at the time have articulated what I was feeling clearly. Only in the last fifteen or so years could I have retroactively explained what I had felt. No one knew how to handle me, and everyone seemed to take different approaches. I didn't know how the adults in my life could have communicated with me in a manner that would have been beneficial. I can only tell you the ones that were the most successful in the end were the ones that approached me from a place of love and understanding.

Our current academic landscape is designed to create order and structure. I don't think initially the schoolhouse was a place where young people were funneled and squeezed through a system designed for the brightest and most obedient children. I think it was a place where education was the goal. Where teachers were teachers, because they had a passion and a gift for it. The best teachers I had, that I remember, are the ones that when they teach you about their given subject, they became animated and fill the room with love and light! The teachers that I tested, and normally on some level broke, were the ones that showed up to chase a paycheck, benefits, or retirement. They were the ones that had long forgotten their "Why's." It wasn't about recognizing who I was or what I needed to excel. If I had been challenged and channeled appropriately, in line with my gifts, my graduating GPA of 1.9 would likely have looked much different.

If you are reading this and thinking, "I know a young person like this!" Let me just say there is hope. It is our responsibility to challenge these young minds and figure out how to meet them where they are. It is essential that we elevate them to their given potential.

I believe that most of my teachers despised me. I think it was because I would calculate within the first couple of weeks how many assignments I could miss. I would calculate what I needed to get on my test in order to pass their class with a C or D. Those calculations dictated my effort. Some of their responses to a student like me were pretty entertaining.

To hit the highlight real, in second grade a had a teacher that constructed a box made of cardboard. She put me in the box, I was forced to do my work in the box. I wasn't allowed to communicate with my fellow students during the course of regular lesson time. She would regularly take away my recess privileges as well. She has a special dark place in the memories of my childhood. It amazes me that she couldn't see how hurt I was, and how much I just needed a hug. I will never forget this teachers name. I have watched as my wait staff has served her and her husband inside of one of my restaurants, all the while wondering if she ever remembers tormenting an already destroyed little boy.

Sixth grade was the first time I had a teacher threaten physical harm to me. Her exact words were, "I want to shove your little head through that locker, but I can't afford to pay my husband to defend me in court!" She was shaking mad! Her little 120 pound frame tensed from head to toe. With fists clenched, this otherwise mild mannered early 60's teacher, was ready to fight me. However, like I said, fear is a feeling that falls pretty dead on me. In those days I didn't feel it at all. So I responded with a slight chuckle, "I can't believe that he would charge you!"

In seventh grade one of the male teachers, who had mistakenly thought I shot a spitball, had to physically be removed by a neighboring teacher when I refused to take the blame for it. I pointed out that the real reason he didn't like me. It was actually, because I didn't find it necessary to answer the same 15 ridiculous questions ever other day. I went on to inform him that he should only explain stuff one time. I also explained that if he spent as much time teaching every class as he did talking with the jocks about basketball, maybe I would be willing to match his effort. **Side-note he was forced to apologize to me in front of the entire class because in this rare instance, I was actually not guilty.

The fact is, my teachers would teach something one time and I got it. Then they would move on, but never fully moving on. There was always a regurgitation of the same things that we've already been taught. The way my mind worked is that once I learned it, there was no need to go over it repetitively. I didn't realize that schools were designed to educate to the slowest person in the room. So for me, I was bored. I got to see the difference between that mentor, that teacher, Mrs. Moore, and my second grade and third grade teachers, my fourth grade teachers, my fifth grade teachers. It allowed me to recognize those special souls that go to school to love first and teach second.

These follies continue on throughout my entire middle and high school career. At the end of the day I was as intelligent as most of the other kids. I just didn't care about school. I cared even less for having to conform to the rules and standards of the other kids around me. I felt like I hadn't heard a single thing that interested me as a young person.

You need to see that every single one of those experiences will give you an opportunity to see beyond the confines of our mental boxes. Regardless of whether or not your childhood was full of caring and loving adults, or if like mine you were the product of a combination of personality types, you can always extract lessons from both the good and bad of your past. Savvy?

Watch and Learn

I had another teacher in high school that really stands out in my mind. Her name was Holly Cassellman. She recognized me for who I was and she recognized me for who I could be. Mrs. Cassellman had a firm hand in the way that she handled her students, which I needed and appreciated. She also took the time to speak into my world. Mrs. Cassellman recognized what I was going through. She downloaded and thought about me specifically as an individual and then spoke into my world. Mrs. Cassellman took the time to understand my situation and did little things that showed me that she cared. She was a great teacher that focused on her students before the content she was teaching. There are lots of other short term mentors that filled a role in my life. Those are just a couple of examples.

I moved out of my parents home when I was 17 years old at the beginning of my senior year. Holly, I started calling her Holly Cassellman after I graduated high school, Mrs. Cassellman at the time, gave me a book, What to Do Now That Mom's Not Around. I don't know why that was on her heart to give me a book. I don't know what made her think that she, you know doing that, would make a difference in my world. Mrs. Cassellman might not even remember that gift today, but for me that book was exactly what I needed. It gave me some nuggets on how to just operate as a fully functioning adult on my own without paternal supervision, without the little things. The book taught how to clean a pan. It offered me just little bits of advice, even how to sew a rip in pants. These were just little things that she assumed somebody wasn't teaching me, and she was absolutely right. That book was such a blessing that came at a terrific time in my life. I'll tell you the biggest thing that I learned from receiving a book that she might or might not remember giving today. I learned the power of giving a gift to someone that could never pay me back. She was a great mentor that took the time to know my situation and lift me to the next level.

This chapter isn't designed to brag about my specific mentors, or how I was a pro at pissing off a bunch of people inside of education. It is designed to demonstrate that you have likely been surrounded by mentors your entire life. It would be a fantastic use of a couple of hours to simply go back and document as many teachers that affected you both positively and negatively. What lessons did you extract that can still serve you today?

Within twelve months of graduating high school, I had opened my first company legally. I also ran a very profitable side line business reprogramming satellite cards to give the holder of the card unlimited channels. I was selling around ten of those a week at $250 each. It was really a great, little less than legal, opportunity until the satellite company figured out what was happening and started sending a kill signal every eighteen minutes. Again, I'm being real. I wasn't perfect. I didn't sit at the feet of Steve Jobs or Bill Gates. I didn't grow up in Silicon Valley with a bunch of super influencers. It isn't a necessary ingredient to your recipe for success.

It has been a valuable lesson that I have taught my daughters. If they want to accelerate faster, amass wealth quicker, be a thought leader, and influencer, then they have to constantly be watching for mentors throughout the educational process. Not only acknowledging key educators as mentors, but also being mindful enough to commit those educator's best lessons into their personal arsenal. I would give you the same advice. Retroactively, go back and see if you can find lessons that have been there all along but never accessed mindfully. Savvy?

I'm An Adult

What do you know?

After high school, I met my wife. We got married very young. Although her father probably wishes, or wished at the time definitely, I don't think anymore, but at the time wished that my wife would have picked someone else. When I met her, I knew what was going to happen, and I pursued her with absolutely everything that I had. She didn't have a chance. I understood strategic seduction. I understood framing conversations. I understood the art of closing. I understood expanding the gap, showing the pain point, closing and bridging the gap. I understood a lot of things in respect to communication and sales. I didn't know what to call these strategies. I didn't understand them as theories or principles, but I understood how to use them. My grandfather and other key mentors in my life up to that point had challenged me, had pushed me to negotiate for everything.

The first group of mentors are relatives that are caring, loving, and very steady, giving, pushing, and sprinting alongside of you. They are challenging you to accelerate as fast as you can. My mother was an example of the second group.

My mother had the best intentions; however, she also had tons of issues. Learning to communicate with her prepared me for every mental obstacle you could imagine. She represents good intentioned relatives that do their very best but challenge you every step of the way. I would ask her if I could go out with my friends. I would even suggest that I would be back at 11 o'clock. No way would my mom let that fly. She would want me home by 9:00. This gave me the perfect opportunity to exercise my negotiation tactics. I would have to talk through all of the points of why it was logical and made sense for me to be allowed to stay out until 11:00 P.M. You think everybody gets to do this, right? Most people accepted the original curfew as that's the rule. My grandfather had taught me that you don't truly want something unless you ask for it at least three times. So, I learned to negotiate. Every single time I wanted something, my mom made me earn it. It was probably the single greatest gift she gave me: not just my mother, but a mentor.

My mother consistently challenging me helped me learn how to communicate. It added to my arsenal, which later in my lifetime, was useful whenever I wanted to pursue a wife that was way out of my league. God knew what I needed in my life, who I needed in my life, what I was manifesting and bringing together. Due to my belief systems and my expectation of my gifting from this role, I fine tuned my communication strategies. Through my wife, I met my father-in-law, who had created multiple businesses. Gene Finch had been in the lumber yard business, the salvage business, and had an assortment of passive income avenues under his belt. A very brilliant, accomplished man and served as probably my second greatest influencer. My father in law recognized something in me that no one else had. Gene acknowledged that spark in me for what it was. He labeled me as an entrepreneur, just like him.

We've now covered family members as mentors. We've covered educators. We've covered chance encounters, in-laws, and other relatives. Let's direct our attention to friends as mentors. Friends are a unique set of mentors, because friends are people who we can align and grow together. In most cases, our peers are our friends. They're in the 33% that hang with us. Every once in a while, you'll become friends with someone that is on a different level, the next level. Sometimes five times or even ten times ahead of where you are currently. These friends will recognize your works, and they will see in you maybe what you see, but maybe not. They might see more in you than you see in yourself at that time. Those friends step in and they become foundational friendships and relationships that'll last an absolute lifetime. Those mentors go beyond business. Guys that will speak into your personal life are invaluable. Often they will teach you about faith. Even better they will teach you how to treat your wife. Hopefully, they will be married and that marriage will teach your wife how to treat her husband. These mentor friends will speak into your life. They know you intimately, and they are strides ahead of you in the game of life. Or maybe they're just, from a wisdom standpoint, light years ahead of you.

My wife and I have a couple that we've known for over a decade now, Dave and Kathy Copeland. They have two wonderful kids, Josh and Jessica. We met this family through our church. We were fortunate enough to join their small group and instantly we were just attracted to their common sense approach to their faith and to family. From the outside looking in, I watched as the Copelands operated. They displayed almost a mafia mentality inside of their family. Loyalty to each other that was so thick and palpable that you couldn't be in the room with them without noticing. It was evident that they were a family that was in love with one another. The Copelands taught us lessons about nearly every category of my life. Dave and Kathy have spoken both into my world and into my wife's world. When they speak, we listen, because we looked at them and recognized they had what we wanted. To us, the Copelands have the perfect family; they truly love and care about others while having total business success.

Life offers pastors, coaches, and lots of different opportunities to meet people that will sharpen you in the area that is their trained expertise. About the same time that we met Dave and Kathy Copeland, we started attending a church in Chillicothe, Missouri, Cornerstone Church. I understand this isn't the path for everybody. This was just our path. This is just my walk, so that you can look. I share these stories with you, not to try to direct you down the same path as me, but instead, to get you thinking about where in your life are incredible mentors hiding in the background. Where in your life can you be seeking mentors. Or like us, when we started attending a non-denominational church we were introduced to the pastoral team. At Cornerstone Church this was a husband and wife team.

Within just a couple three years, those pastors stopped being our pastors and started to be our friends. We had built such a strong relationship with them that our conversations became very two-way. As I accelerated in business, we would talk about our business ventures. I would talk to the husband about the business of church. When I needed help and reassurance in faith-based mentoring, I knew I could pick up the phone and give the pastor a call. He would freely and gladly give me his time, to a point that he would drive from the church to my office and spend time with me. The two of us spent hours talking about life, balance, family, business, and God's word.

Never underestimate the people who are in your world right now offering up sage wisdom. The main litmus test for you should be what we talked about earlier in the book. What does this person have to gain from their advice? Then finally, is that little voice inside of me agreeing or screaming "RUN!"? Savvy?

Pay to Play

Finally, paid mentors. Paid mentors can be the greatest asset or the greatest waste that you can pursue inside of this entire mentor conversation. I have paid several different mentors. All of them I've been extremely mindful, careful, and heavily researched before I wrote a single check. I needed to make sure that what they were teaching was exactly what I needed to fill my life and fill my void. When you think about business as your body and all of the body's moving parts, you'll focus on certain body parts. Whenever you're lifting weights trying to build out or trying to slim down there are different strategies to proceed. You might recognize, man my legs are a little weaker than my upper body. I need to focus on legs. Now in the world of business, it's no different. I'm really great at marketing, but I suck at my family life right now. Or I'm really great inside of my physicality, but my business is really struggling. Whatever the case may be, you find mentors that fill those specific gaps.

When there's a skill set or something that you feel is necessary for you to be able to step into and grow, to add to that muscle base inside that part of your business, those are the mentors that you pursue. Just as a little drop of advice from me, being able to communicate about a subject does not make someone qualified to be a mentor. Being able to post a

Facebook advertisement does not qualify somebody to be a mentor. A mentor is someone that has been in the battlefield in the center of the trenches. A true mentor will understand the fight. A business mentor will understand what it takes to win. They've been down the path. The specific muscle group that you are trying to build, they have done before, and they have done it successfully.

For me, I've got three different guys that have really stood out in my mind that I have paid considerable amounts of money. I am talking about spending hundreds of thousands of dollars. The first guy, which I spoke about earlier, Wake Up Warrior, Garrett White, was that first mentor that I needed. Garrett's insights and wisdom in respect to what he calls the having it all lifestyle, was exactly what I needed. Although I felt that I had pinnacled in life at the time, I was miserable. Back then, I didn't recognize what it was that I needed to embrace to step out into power again and sprint toward my next business success. Garrett White was exactly what I needed. His team of coaches will forever have a special place in my heart. A couple of those guys I stay in communication with every single day.

Secondly, Russell Brunson is one of my personal mentors. I mentioned him briefly almost in a jab manner earlier. Russell's material and Russell's software service platform is brilliant. What Russell has created to allow people to communicate is over the top. He allows penetration deep into the internet and into social platforms to present yourself or your skill set as a product or a service is brilliant. The way Russell communicates via his digital marketing is next level. A friend of mine, named Jacob Hiller. Jacob created the jump manual before anybody knew what a click funnel was. He produced an e-book on how to slam dunk a basketball. If you've never heard of Jacob Hiller or don't follow him online yet, go ahead and do that right now. His Instagram is @Jacobwh. Hiller is a brilliant guy that introduced me to click funnels long before I was ready for that to even be something that I was interested in. When the time was right, the skills were in place, the muscles were weak in that marketing area and today's internet economy, I needed to step up my game. So, Russell was the perfect mentor for me.

I signed up for a big package Russell Brunson offered. I went through every bit of material and content available. I took notes about every book that he had written. I signed up in one of his coaching programs. Yeah, the rest is history. Brilliant information from the legend, Russell Brunson.

Finally, and most recently, I paid to travel to New York City, the Big Apple. I took time out of building my automotive dealership to meet and train with Gary Vaynerchuk and his brilliant team. They have a program called the Four D's out at Vayner Media. Basically, the Four D's is a daily digital deep dive that lets you as an entrepreneur come and sit at the table with Gary and his team. The Vaynerchuck team basically reads you their entire playbook of how they're marketing in today's digital landscape. Most everybody who's reading this book will know who Gary Vaynerchuk is. If you don't, what rock have you been living under? Here's his information. **@garyvee** Go check him out. This guy's an absolute powerhouse.

Here's the crazy part. The first time that I paid a mentor, I paid $100 a session. The last mentor program that I trained with cost me $15,000 for an eight hour session. You are probably thinking to yourself, Why would he do that? I would ask you, Why aren't you already doing that? The reason I'm doing it, the reason I'll continue to do it, is because these guys cause me to level up. Mentors have the ability to grab you by the wrist and rip you from the crab trap if you'll ask them. If you'll sacrifice to pay them, and if you'll do what they tell you to do. Period. Dot. The end.

Most books that I've picked up are written about self-help. Many are written about business. Others are written to accelerate wealth. Frequently these authors write about revolutionary concepts that claim to accelerate a company while helping to progress to the next level, are full of a bunch of fluff. Typically, there's one or two very good concepts inside of a book. These nuggets give the illusion that possibly there's a revelation inside that I need to open my mind and investigate. These books might even present a scenario that I hadn't considered. When I read I am looking for a different view or perspective of something I've already known or that I've heard but I've never been able to apply. I read to see if I am missing a concept that I've never been able to take to heart and effectively use across all areas of my life. Savvy?

Readers Are Leaders

This brings me to the last category of mentors. This category may be the greatest and the most vast. One guy I want to mention is Ty Lopez, a modern day digital tycoon. Ty has built the foundation of his social influencing career around one concept. That concept is books allow you to be mentored by the greatest minds in history. I truly believe that's so extremely true. You've heard this saying, readers are leaders, for a reason. It sounds cliché and it sounds like a bunch of mumbo jumbo. However, that's an easy thing to say when you're sitting on the sideline judging why your life hasn't excelled or accelerated at the pace at which you expect. If your life is not at the pace that you see others gaining by leaps and bounds, it might be time to pick up a book written by a terrific mentor that will change your path.

You see, I mentioned earlier I barely graduated high school with a 1.9 GPA. In high school I understood C's and D's got degrees. The only degree I was interested in getting was my high school diploma. I desperately wanted to break free of that institution. I recognized that no one would hire me without a diploma. Although I never had long-term intentions of working for the other man, I recognized that I would, at some point, need a job. So I stuck it out in high school. My father had dropped out of high school and my mother had dropped out of middle school. My father got his GED and my mother eventually did too when she was about 30 years old. She went on to get her CNA and helped a lot of people. It was one of the greatest praises that I ever got about my mother, actually. Someone mentioned to me that my mother had been a blessing to this man's mother in her final days. That his mother had looked forward to the days that my mother would walk into the room and make her life a little bit better. I say this because sometimes being rich can be a measure of the impact you have in the world. Impacting others was as rich as she would ever be.

For me, high school was just an institution, a crab trap, a cage, something that I didn't find interesting. I felt like they had taught us the gross portion of the principles in school by the time we were in 8th grade and 9th, 10th, 11th, and 12th were regurgitation of the lessons they had taught us earlier. I recognize now, as an adult, my thinking wasn't true. My mentality set the pace for my ability to uptake in that environment but it wasn't for me. When I got out of school, I began to read. I read because my peers in business were sharper than me. My peers in business knew concepts I didn't. They had theories and they had things that they could apply to different scenarios that I had never heard of. I wanted to learn everything from branding, marketing, advertising, all the way to distribution. I felt like I was not as equipped as others in my field. I sat in a meeting once, and I felt like the dumbest man at the table. I left that meeting and thought I will never feel that way again. So I began to read.

I read absolutely anything on any subject regarding business and money. I've read books about accounting. I've read books about strategy. I've read books about marketing. I've read books about sales, closing, distribution, and organizational structure. I've read books about human resources. I've read books about getting rich, investing in real estate, investing in stocks, and the Forex market. If I wanted to know something about a subject, if I wanted to be able to speak clearly and be respected amongst my peers in a conversation, I realized that I had to increase my human bandwidth. The only way to do that is through mentorship and reading.

There's a really great quote that I quite enjoy. It goes something like this, the only difference between a man today and a man one year from now is who he knows and what he's read. I find that quote so incredibly true for my life. You have an opportunity to be mentored by the greatest minds in the world. It's probably the single largest driver for me to write this book. I am hoping that it reaches people and mentors the people that I can't physically get to. I want this book to give somebody the courage to step out. I want to equip people to do the thing that I was blessed with the opportunity to do, to have the things that I've been blessed with in this lifetime. It is my responsibility to help others to excel to a point that right now they can only dream about. So, if you truly want to be mentored by the very best in all of the world, pick up a book and read. Savvy?

I Might Be Your Sensei

It could seem like a lead up to, "Hi, I'm Michael and you should pay me to help you!" And you are thinking something like, "Here is the ask! I knew he was going to try to sell me something! Ha, I am so right!" The truth is you just have a skewed thought process when it comes to money. I'm not trying to sell you on blowing money. I am simply trying to get you to realize this game is no different from anything else in this world. There are people who have amassed decades of knowledge in the world of business. Many people expect successful entrepreneurs to share their knowledge, most of us are willing to coach and guide others. However, it is a time commitment on your part, and it shouldn't be free! One mentor can shave twenty years off of your learning curve. This allows you to have an edge that will save you not only time but also money. I might be the perfect person to help you bridge the gap when it comes to your next career or business move. The chances are that I am probably not the right guy for most of the people reading this book. However, for a small percentage of you I might be the perfect person to help you 10X your life!

I found myself as a little kid living vicariously through television and movies. I thought that if I could find a group of friends to run down the tracks with me, we would defiantly find a dead body! I was certain that there really was a never ending story and someday I would ride the back of a 40 ft long talking dog that could fly. I was willing to look behind my clothes seeking that secret door that would let me find Narnia. Recently I was scrolling through Instagram and a trailer for a new YouTube movie sent me shooting back to some of my funnest childhood memories. The trailer is for a show called Cobra Kai. The other side of the Karate Kid story. I remember always wanting to learn karate. I knew that I could be good at it, and I also new that it would take lessons. Lessons cost money, and when it came to my parents investing in their children that wasn't a possibility. So I not only watched every Karate Kid movie there was, I mastered every scene of ever one of the movies. I believed that if I could master *wax on, wax off,* that I could be a blackbelt in karate! One day in the backyard I "crane kicked" about a dozen boards out of our privacy fence! Enter the next TV learned lesson 'Ninja Vanish!"

The lesson is simple, I could have watched every karate movie ever made. I could have practiced out in my yard, I could have believed that I was capable. I even could have suckered the kids in my neighborhood into believing that I was a karate expert. However, without a sensei I was just a poser. I needed someone who was experienced at karate to not only teach me but to guide my movements, encourage me through my struggles, and reenforce my God given strengths.

In the art of business, you need to find your sensei. You should pay them whatever they ask. Finally, you should trust their processes. You may find yourself thinking why in the world am I waxing this car? How does this help me? Then one day you realize that your ability to *wax on, wax off* can save you from being punched in the face! Savvy?

Prime the Machine

The next few chapters are longer than most. I want you to associate very closely with the combined lesson inside of the next few chapters. I feel as though there is a balance of me sharing with you what has worked for me as well as what lessons are to be found that we can all benefit. It would be easy to think, I know how to work out so I think I will skip this chapter. Don't do it. You will find so much power through understanding how to use physicality as a wealth building tool. Let's get after it!

Your body is a temple. In order to be successful in all areas of life, you must start with yourself. There are three main keys to our physicality that will increase your likelihood of success in all areas of your life: 1. Fuel 2. Resistance 3. Rest.

If you want to operate in the greatest place of power possible, then you need to be mentally and physically prepared. I think I can sum up this concept in one brief explanation:

Your ability to mentally and physically tackle any task placed in front of you will be directly tied to your capacity. Your capacity is to not only deal with the immediate pressure of the situation, but also your clarity to see the situation for what it is. That clarity gives you the fortitude to fight, however long is necessary without giving up before the task is complete.

This sounds simple, right? Well sort of, let me explain. In other words, you need to be clear minded (rested), you need to be able to mentally push through your own internal desires (resistance), and finally you need to be able to perform at a high level for extensive periods of time (fueled).

At the end of the day it's about personal goals. When you look at me, you might notice that I am not going to get a call any time soon to be shirtless on the cover of Muscle Mag or anywhere else for that matter. I simply eat and work out in a way that keeps me feeling good about myself. Working out and eating clean allows my daily energy to outpace my mental burn rate. Think of it like a battery in a remote control car. When the battery is powered above 50%, there is a noticeable difference in the way the car operates. It operates at its peak performance. In the simplest most basic way, you should train your body to run like a machine. It is one little thing you can absolutely control regardless of the storms you are facing with your business, family, relationships or your other interests. This is the one thing in your life that you have 100% control over. So, in short take control of it today. Make a personal commitment to step into the lowest hanging fruit when it comes to obtaining sustainable power in all areas of your life, your personal temple. It's time to clean up your house. Savvy?

Sleep.

The tortoise and the hare is a lie!

Iwill let you in on a secret, until you have enough money to singularly focus on your desires you will need enough energy to grind from dusk until dawn. If you are serious about building wealth, then you have to be willing to grind harder than anyone you know. One of my greatest mentors was my father-in-law. It didn't take long for him and I to realize that we were a pretty powerful team in business. He introduced me to the real-estate market and taught me how to look at properties with a new set of educated eyes. I have made hundreds and thousands of dollars in real estate because of his advice. Although it is not my primary focus, my largest real estate purchase to date was around $1.5M, and that property generates $141K a year. Granted, real estate has been good for me it is not the focus of this book. I only mention real estate to say that I am going to share with you the single greatest piece of advice my father in law ever gave me! Thats right, this information is worth way more than my real estate gains. In order for you to capitalize on this golden nugget you will need to treat your body like it is a temple. You will have to maintain it. You will have to fuel it. You will have to have it rested. Also, you will have to be willing to sacrifice copious amounts of sleep to execute it.

I had watched my grandfather get up anywhere from 4:00 AM - 5:00 AM my entire childhood. My grandfather and one of my uncles had decided to get into the hog business. His beautiful barn style home sat in the middle of the thirty acre farm, mostly fenced in and full of pigs. He would get up in the morning, read the paper, and drink his coffee. Within thirty minutes of him getting out of bed, we were headed out the door to feed the pigs and make sure nothing was out of order or broken. On a normal morning, he was loading his lunchbox along with his old green thermos full of coffee into the old farm truck to head off to work. He would work and typically not get back home until around 5:30 PM. For most people they would say to themselves, "Well, I am working two different jobs, I deserve a break." That is not the millionaire mindset. It doesn't fit what I watched my grandfather do my entire childhood. It doesn't fit what I remember my dad doing to get ahead and exit the rat race.

Additionally, it doesn't align with that advice my father in law gave me that made the light come on for me. His words were simple but profound, "Michael if you truly want to be wealthy I am going to tell you the secret." It was what he had done his entire life. He didn't think anything of it. Once your mind is programmed that this is how you operate, it will simply set you in the fast lane. Period. He said,"Go to work to pay your bills, just like everyone else does. Unlike the general population of workers, if you want to really make money, you have to make it in the nights and on the weekends!"

At first I thought "Forget that, I need… Scratch that, I deserve my time off! I work hard, he doesn't get how much I work. He is just old school. That won't work for me. My wife will get mad. I will miss my family. My kids need me to be there with them…" I had at least 509 additional stories just like those. Ignorant lies that gave me permission to be lazy.

It could easily seem like I'm digressing in this chapter. Regardless, I want to make it very clear to you, if you are over weight, if your mind is sluggish, if you are like me and have trouble focussing for long periods of time, you will have to get your body physically prepared for the additional hours it will take for you to work on your side hustles. Otherwise you will finish your 40 hour a week gig and be too physically and mentally exhausted to pursue anything else! I want to be extremely clear about this. I am not suggesting that if you are overweight you can't be successful! Your visual physicality is not the conversation. Rather, your fitness is an exercise of the mind. You have to be able to bust through some barriers mentally if you want to make it to your first million! Savvy?

Lets take a minute to talk about a couple of the other benefits to being physically fit. I have watched at least a hundred different people that I know begin to gain a bit of success at work and inevitably they get sucked into their business. Often they find themselves grinding out 60-80 hours a week. One of the first things they let go is their body. Why is that the case? Think about when you felt the best about yourself. Think back, is it when you had the most money, is it when you got that new job, promotion, commission? Probably not, unless it is tied to when you physically felt your best. Every time I have absolutely felt like I could crush the world it was because I physically felt like a million bucks! Can you gain wealth and be in poor physical shape? Yes, of course you can, but why would you ever want to? This is your one chance. You get one at bat at this life, what do you expect from it?

I love old gangster movies. One of my favorite scenes in any movie ever is when Al Paccino (Tony Mantano) was asked, "Tony, what do you want?" His response is what I believe our goal should be. He smiled and said, "The world chico and everything in it!" I'm not saying we should pursue literally everything. However, if something is on your heart, whether it is material, relational, physical or spiritual, I believe you can obtain it and you should be able to. The only question is are you willing to do the work necessary to EARN it? This world won't give you anything. If you want something you have to go take it. Who doesn't want to look and feel good? Who doesn't want to have relationships where you aren't held back by physicality? Who doesn't want to be able to have amazing sexual relationships with your significant other because you feel physically on fire? Why would you ever choose to slug through this life when you can live it on fire and in total power?! Savvy?

I Hate Running

And Other Tales

I think if I tried real hard I could probably remember the first time I ran a mile. Even as a young person if I was just trying to run for the sake of running, I would push myself too hard and gas out. I couldn't continue to run because physically I just hadn't conditioned myself for it. With my failed attempts at running a mile, I began to tell myself a story that I was not physically fit. I'm not that strong. You see, I was pretty skinny. So in looking at me visually, you would think, "This guy's a runner." However, the fact is that I was hardly a runner. I hadn't conditioned myself to run more than a short sprint.

Being physically fit intrigued me from a young age. I wanted to be strong and in shape. Therefore, I would get on a 3, 4, 5-day kick of working out. I would decide that I was going to lift weights and get strong. In my mind, if I did those things I could start on the football team, or I could become a wrestler. Whatever sport sparked my interest at the time regarding being fit was usually not enough to hold my interest. Whatever my whimsical desire was that week, I would pursue it with a whimsical pursuit. Going up into the weight room would result in me doing the lifts that felt natural to me. Of course I gravitated toward lifts that made me feel strong. In the gym I would do stuff like the calf raise machine or the lat pull down machine. These exercises I could do without enhancing how weak I truly was. It was extremely discouraging for me to even grace the door of the weight room. Naturally, I avoided the more basic lifts. You would not have caught me doing dead lifts. Heaven forbid me to try weighted squats. The bench press was extremely intimidating. In my mind the worst thing about a gym was cardiovascular activity. You would NEVER catch me doing any of that, EVER!

Most of the people who are reading this have kind of figured out where you are physically. If being in shape physically is not easy for you, then we are similar. I have to work to obtain the physical strength that I feel is mandatory for me to be successful. At this point, you need to look in the mirror for an honest self evaluation. You may think your body is on fire and I'm right where I need to be, or you may look in the mirror and think I'm not where I want to be yet. Either way, you are the deciding factor in your physical appearance. It is completely up to you.

A self evaluation is essential. No one else will be completely honest with you. If you're completely broken down when you look in the mirror because of your physical attributes, that is okay. It gives you a starting point. If you think your body looks like total crap and you hate to look at yourself, then it is time to make a change. Truly assessing where you are visually is important. Don't allow your mental track to switch to something that's more palpable, something that doesn't require you to listen to that nagging voice in the back of your head that is screaming for change. I know that you really do want to be the best version of yourself that is possible! Do not allow your mind to wander onto easier subjects like: What do I have going on today? What do the kids want me to do? What's the wife got planned for me? The fact is this; the very healthiest thing you can do is look in the mirror and realize exactly where you are today. Ask yourself if you are someplace physically that puts you in a position of power?

This isn't a short chapter because it is vital to your success. You need to truly understand how your physicality affects your pursuit of greatness. For me, I'm not trying to be a body builder. I'm not trying to be a marathon runner. I'm not trying to be a power lifter. I don't think that I have any chance ever of being a male fitness model. I am your average 200-210 pound, a little on the bigger build, guy. I can run a couple miles. I can bench press 225 extremely consistently. I can dead lift between 350 and 400 pounds, and I can squat somewhere around 250 to 300. This data about myself helps me to set goals and pursue the best me possible. It literally sets me up for success every day.

I'm only sharing these statistics with you because I don't think that you have to choose to be obsessed with your physicality. Working out puts you in a position of power that allows you to have the ability to push yourself physically in order to defeat that little weak voice in your mind. What do I mean by that? Your mind has the ability to literally walk through any fire. However, in our life beginning with the time that we were extremely small our parents catered to our every whimsical scream and cry, want, and desire. If we cried they were quick to pacify us. If we showed any kind of discomforted emotions as we grow up, the people around us want us to shut up, so they fix it. They don't want a crying 3-year-old in the room. Most people have the mentality to give that kid what they want or scold them and teach them to swallow those desires and make the noise disappear. The problem is that as young people grow into adults they are rarely retaught this lesson and the crying baby voice in the back of their head grows stronger and stronger. As they progress through life they grow and get older, they do the same thing. They cry for what they want, but that weak little voice gets a new trick. It learns to pacify itself with lies! Your mind builds a mechanism that is programmed like this: if I can't get what I want, then I create a story that justifies why I can't get it. The voice now starts telling you lies. Lies like: It's never my fault. Whatever is bothering you is never the result of your own actions, always the result of someone else's. The consequences you are facing are always the result of the economy, the weather, John did this, Jane did that, even Sally never gave me a chance.

You are likely wondering how does this have anything to do with my physicality? It's simple. Every time you push yourself in a workout, you break that weak voice down more and more. Soon the stronger voice in your head replaces the lies with truths. As you continuously stomp that weaker voice out through pushing yourself physically, you will notice the stronger voice in your head replacing lies with truths. Normally, it is the same simple truth. "I didn't accomplish that, or I didn't obtain that because of me. No one else is responsible for my shortcomings. It's no one's fault but mine!" Your mind, because you've been conditioned to operate this way your entire life, is now broken. Your mind prevents you from walking through discomfort. Your mind prevents you from walking through pain. Your mind prevents you from being willing to track through whatever it is that you've got going on in your life.

God gives us these amazing gifts. Although, many of the gifts that we've been given aren't visually scalable. Our bodies, inside of this conversation, are externally scalable. Unfortunately most people exercise their body for vanity instead of power. When you're working out, you need to push yourself mentally to a place that you're miserable. The entire point of the misery isn't to physically look like a specimen, but instead train your mind. Your mind needs to be trained to walk through discomfort and not to quit early. You must work to train your body to get through to the other side of the discomfort to the reward of success. You see in the conversation of scale, business, and the wealthy, your objective is to be able to walk through the fire and come out successful on the other side.

Working out becomes a vehicle to exercise a muscle that you can't see. Working out becomes a vehicle to exercise your will, your heart, and your mind's capacity to disconnect to the discomforts of our body. Working out increases your ability to work past the discomforts of the stories and accomplish whatever goal you set your mind to. Foundationally, this is an area that you must master. There will be road blocks. I had stories. When I was a small child the story I thought was I can't run, and I'm not very strong. Those were stories that blocked me from moving forward to make progress.

It wasn't until much later in life that I realized that if I could squash the stories, I could accelerate my growth. Most of my mentors, my close inner circle mentors aren't physical specimens of masculinity. My grandfather, as we talked about lots of times, was a worker. However, even until he was dying at the age of 87, he was a thin man. Grandpa was 6'2" and weighed somewhere around 150-160 pounds. At his heaviest weight of his life maybe he got up to 175 pounds.

I don't know if my grandfather in the last 50 years of his life spent one day inside of a weight room or a gym. I do know that every single day he was outside working and grinding physically. The military had given him the fortitude mentally to understand objectives and to disconnect his own emotional desires. The military also taught him to persevere regardless of what he felt internally and to disconnect to what he felt emotionally. You'll find that a lot of soldiers have the ability to do the work that no one else wants to do. Most military soldiers can accomplish success without complaining, because they've been broken from this mental capacity of incompletion of a task. They are not capable of functioning at a level of doing only what feels good.

Another mentor that I have, I've not seen in the gym. I've never seen my father-in-law workout. In the last 20 years of my relationship with him, he's taught me multitudes about business and multitudes about discipline. He smoked cigarettes early in his lifetime. Fortunately, the second that the Surgeon

General came out with a warning on the side of the pack about cigarettes giving you cancer, he wadded up and threw that half a pack of cigarettes in the trash. He had the discipline to never smoke again.

Drinking was the same way for my father in law. He decided somewhere in his 40s that drinking alcohol wasn't good for him. He decided that he wasn't going to do it again. He had the mental fortitude to resolve that this doesn't benefit me in my goals. He realized that cigarettes and alcohol were stumbling blocks between him and his goals. What were his goals you ask? His goals were to build extreme wealth and to live a long fulfilling life.

This is what exercise does for you. Exercise builds the platform for you to have the mental fortitude to accomplish whatever your goal may be. Exercise causes you to have discipline in your life. It causes you to push past the uncomfortable feelings. You may have soreness, but you must persevere. You might want to quit, but you must persevere. You might be injured, but you must persevere. You might be crazy busy, but you must persevere. You owe it to yourself to learn to defeat that weak little voice that you have been a slave to the greater part of your life. Exercise expands your mind and your vision in a necessary way for success.

You may have stumbling blocks in your life between you and your goals. Maybe you need to quit smoking or maybe you need to lose weight. Both of these things are mentally and physically taxing. If you succumb to every whimsical desire that you have internally, you'll never scale to a point in any level of wealth. This is a harsh reality that is difficult to accept.

Now you might be thinking, Michael I know some fat guys who smoke and who are extremely wealthy. Absolutely that can happen. However, is that helping you reach your goals? The object of what we are doing through this walk is stacking the deck in your favor. I want you set up for success. You might have a superpower that can add so much value to the marketplace, that the marketplace will make you rich. I am trying to help you take down the roadblocks to enable you to rocket to your next level.

You might be like me and be able to communicate yourself into and out of any situation. I have the ability to negotiate at whatever level required in a situation to produce. For me communication is my ultimate superpower. My physicality isn't my superpower. However, my physicality is where I stretch and stress my mental fortitude. My physical preparation in the gym prepares me to walk into a difficult situation and not be gassed. The physical stamina that I work for in the gym allows me to have the mental fortitude to endure through any situation. I have the capability to not allow the rhythmic increase of my heart to cause me to be out of breath when I'm giving a keynote speech to an unforgiving audience.

I see so many presentors struggle as they're settling into their comfort zone inside of a public speaking forum. They seem like they're out of breath the first three or four paragraphs of their speech. They haven't been able to disconnect their mental ability from the physical angst of being in discomfort. This all ties back to why creating an environment for your body that taxes it is so important.

Garret J. White with Wake Up Warrior says, "Sweat every day. Get your body in power." Nevertheless, I want you to understand this concept deeper and have a clear understanding of why. Sweating everyday represents the action of moving. It represents your willingness to deny that weak voice in your mind and crush your goals. I have said this already, but I need it to sink in for you. Write this in the margin, or in the front of the book. Post it on social media. Tell a friend. Do whatever you have to do to engrain this concept in your mind. The most important benefit of pushing yourself physically isn't something that you can see. Your success truly comes from learning to defeat the little voice in your mind. If you want to 10X the likely hood of you obtaining wealth or busting through that thing that is holding you back, learn and apply this lesson.

Why do successful people always look so good? Physically if you notice that most people who are extremely wealthy, not who make a good living, but people who have a high, high net worth, why do they physically look so fit? It's because there's a direct correlation to our physicality and our mental fortitude. Successful people make time to take care of their personal temple.

So what does being healthy do for us? I think that for me, and for most people in my inner circle, being physically fit removes one of the stresses and pressures from our world. We recognize that our physicality is one of the pillars of our success. It's the easiest win we can get every single day. Savvy?

Crossfit

Learn To Move The Weight

I enjoy being a member of the Crossfit community. Am I trying to win the Crossfit games? No way. Am I trying to compete at a high level, crushing everyone else in the box? Not at all. My goal is simply to push myself to a level of discomfort. My main objective is to keep myself at that level of discomfort, until I accomplish the WOD (Workout Of the Day). I mark that little check mark of victory at the end of every WOD, and then I go on about the rest of my day. Sometimes reminding myself of that victory as my day goes into the toilet, because you inevitably will have lots of those days that everything feels like it is derailing.

I gain power in my day by reminding myself in those moments, hey, I've already had a victory today. This isn't any harder than what I went through this morning. Focus on what's happening. Separate the problem. Tackle the goal and see it through to the end.

Using my Crossfit example, the weight typically is the problem. A typical WOD requires some heavy lifting. Here is an example of a WOD I have completed recently. It starts with overhead squats at 135 pounds, 20 times. The next move is to run 400 meters. Finally we end with doing some pull ups. Guess what we do next? You guessed it, we repeat the set! We end up doing this same routine for 5 rounds and a timed score. The times are posted for all to see at the gym.

That particular WOD was a challenge. The 135 pound weight inside of the overhead squat is the problem for me. The weight that I carry throughout the run is the problem. The weight that I'm pulling up over the bar is the problem. I have to recognize that I have three different problems in the course of action and it's a pretty consistent fight to get through to the end goal. Do that five times and call it a day. What was my time? Next time I have the same problem, can I do it quicker?

Now, take that exact same analogy and apply it over to business. You have an unhappy customer. Someone is discontent with the product or service that you've offered or that your company has offered. The struggle from the Crossfit analogy applies perfectly in business.

What's the weight in this situation? The weight is the customer's unhappy. Where are you? You are in a miserable spot, because whether customers want to believe it or not, theres not an entrepreneur in the world who goes through what we go through without caring about the customer. Moving the customer from a point of frustration to a place of satisfaction is the WOD. The same as a workout, the more times you do it, the easier it becomes and your time might even get better too!

I've had some customers imply that businesses just care about money and at the end of the money we're done. But that is simply not true. The customers happiness is one of our weights. Entrepreneurs like myself, truly care about people, their customers, and the happiness of the customer.

Do we care about making money? Absolutely we care about the almighty dollar. Is that one of the weights? It absolutely is. The functionality of our team and our team's success individualized or as a group is as top priority. We look at our team and that is the weight. Are they happy? Are they making enough money? Are they fulfilling their role inside of the machine that I've built? For some of you it's just as simple as, does my team even show up consistently? For some of you right now, the weight is I need to create a team. Owning your own operation will cause all of these things to tax you.

Being a business owner will cause all of these things to stress your body. All of these things will stress your mind. All of these things will add pressure to you as you build them. As your company grows, so does the pressure. As you reach higher and higher levels so does the urgency. Why in the world wouldn't you ever work out your physical body? Why wouldn't you push yourself hard in a workout to a point of almost physical exhaustion? A physical breakdown may not seem like a vacation, but the benefits you will gain from it are tremendous. Not because it's an exercise of the body, but because it's an exercise of both the mind and the spirit.

You have to choose to operate inside of power. That power comes from rolling out of bed and starting your day correctly. That power comes when you push your body to a point of discomfort and keep it there for a period of time first thing in the morning. I'm gonna give you some benchmarks, some things that I look for inside of my physical capacity, just as a benchmark to keep me on point. I haven't 100% reached these goals to the fullest, but this is my pursuit. This is a little bit beyond what my current reach is. However, these have scaled and pushed further and further out over the last several years as I've realized how mentally I can push myself to the point of exhaustion. I can push myself to a point of failure and still maintain a level of being able to track my progress.

For me, running represents my cardiovascular capability. I enjoy running. When I'm in terrible shape I can run two miles in about 20 minutes. My goal typically is to be able to run two miles in 16 minutes or less. That puts a 7-something pace on a mile. Every single person who's done any running knows that's never gonna win any kind of race. Being able to run allows me to get up just about any flight of stairs without being out of breath at the top of them. I can go on any kind of a hike or a walk that I want. I have the ability to carry on a conversation while I am moving up a mountain or flight of stairs. I will not struggle physically throughout the course of my day in any kind of capacity that I'm called to operate.

Therefore, my suggestion for you is to set the benchmark. Go for a run. Two miles is enough of a distance that when you're on the run you will be to the point where you have high levels of discomfort. You will feel discomfort especially if you're pushing yourself to set up what I would call your qualifying time. Once you get there, look at your individual miles and set a forward looking goal of thirty seconds less than both of those. Ninety days is plenty of time to take thirty seconds off of each mile. So if your first mile is a nine minute and fifteen second mile and your second mile is a ten minute and twenty second mile, then you've gathered the data to set your ninety day goals. In ninety days you're next mile set should be eight minutes and forty five seconds and nine minutes and fifty seconds respectively. Will it happen without hard work and discomfort? No, you have to put in the work and be willing to be uncomfortable while you are retraining your mind and body to push through the run.

Next, I want to make sure that I'm physically strong. I want to feel like I'm in power. You can set across from someone negotiating at a table and feel like you're pudgy. This happens to many entrepreneurs that are just getting started because in today's entrepreneurial climate a lot of people really grasp the physicality side. Being fit is becoming more and more a part of the entrepreneurs culture. The people who are performing at high levels recognize that this is something that you have to do. So lots of time you'll sit at a conference table with physical specimens of extreme fitness levels. The very last thing you want is a tinge in the back of your mind, a question about your physicality.

It doesn't matter exactly where you are physically, as long as you are continuously improving. It's much more important that you be in a place where you're in power. This doesn't work for everyone but for me this is where I choose to be. I have definitive goals. When I meet them, I will set new goals. I always need to be pushing for more.

These numbers shift and grow as I shift and grow. Take wherever you are and create a benchmark. Then push yourself to a 15% increase beyond where you are currently. That will be your next target. Give yourself ninety days to six months to push as hard as you can towards that target. You will make forward strides. Some days it will not feel like you are making progress. Continue pushing toward your goal anyway. As you change your benchmarks to improve your physical body, this will cause you to have a mental breakthrough in the gym. If you're happy where you are physically strength wise, then your next push is cardio. Wherever you are currently, the point is simple, destroy your body physically in the gym so that you can breakthrough that bridge or mindset of mental failure when you're tracking ahead inside of business. Savvy?

Routine is King

A story that I told myself when I was younger, was that I was hyperactive. This was confirmed not just by my own mind, but also by the adults around me. My mother and other people who were around would say, "Oh, Michael's hyperactive. Michael has the inability to focus for very long, to pay attention to what's going on around him. Michael isn't a good listener. Micheal isn't a good student. Michael is this, Michael is that."

It was a continuous onslaught of speaking this disease, this plethora of negativity over top of me. To the point that I just believed them. I'm hyperactive; I don't have to sit still very long. Oh Michael, you can put him in a corner, and he'll find a piece of dirt to play with. Next time I'm put in a corner, I'm playing with a piece of dirt, because that's what was spoken over me. I had risen to the level of expectation and fulfilled the words spoken over me.

At least that is who I was during the week. The young man I was during the week was entirely different from who I was on the weekends. Like I've mentioned already, I would get off the bus sometime around 3:30. Between 3:30 and 4:00, my grandfather would be parked in front of my house ready to pick me up, whisk me off, and take me to some level of normalcy. For me, grandpa's house was the perfect environment that would allow me to be the best version of myself through routine and through systematic controls.

For example, my grandfather didn't have TV in his home. Therefore, I wasn't filling my mind or my time with a void of nonsensical television. I didn't need the TV to survive. I found out that reading was something that I enjoy doing very much inside of grandpa's home. I also found out that silence wasn't the worst thing in the world. In fact, silence allowed me to flex my imagination. A skill that serves me still today. I found out that just sitting at a dinner table and eating with your family will instill values into your life that you can't teach or preach into life.

I learned that taking the actions and going through the motions are some of the only ways to accomplish the goals that you have. For my grandfather, he had aggressive goals inside of his career and inside of businesses. He had a job. He got up early every morning. He began hustling long before he had to leave for work. Once he got home, he would carve out a little bit of free time. He would have some dinner, maybe go do a little bit of fishing, but there was always an area inside of his evening where he implemented a routine. Whether he would go work in the hog lot, go mow a cemetery, or cut wood, Grandpa was always systematically carving time out to be productive in all areas of his life.

It was his responsibility. However, it wasn't work, it was the routine; it was just what he did. He had to go through the motions of doing the things that were put in front of him as a responsibility. Grandpa was the most dependable man in my world.

Sharing with you the alternative life I was exposed to at my moms house is something that I think is so critical. I need you to recognize that chaos begets chaos and routine begets success. Let me map out a day in the life of Michael as a young child in my mothers home. I'm going to show you how drastically small shifts can influence a young person. It will definitely shine a light on the end result for you. Don't fall into the trap of thinking, "Sure but Michael I'm an adult, it's not the same." Actually it is exactly the same. Children will show us how we are influenced emotionally by external factors. Maybe slightly more subtly but the same on some level.

Let's use Saturday as an example. I lived inside of a home with five brothers and sisters, a home with two parents, a home with a lot of chaos, a home without a lot of recreational things to do. This would be a typical Saturday, that for some reason, I was unable to spend the weekend with my Grandpa.

I found myself impacted by a number of outside influences. First and foremost what time did I wake up at home? Normally for me, I would wake up anytime between 7 AM and 10 AM. There wasn't a set time that you get out of bed, and there was no reason to get out of bed early. Typically, I was getting out of bed whenever I was being bothered by a family member, or whenever one of my brothers or sisters wanted me to come play, or I would hear a noise from another part of the house. An example of this is someone would turn on the TV, and it would be up too loud.

I would typically crawl out of bed. There wasn't a routine of go right to the bathroom and brush my teeth, get cleaned up, and start my day. That just wasn't the culture inside of my home. It wasn't something that was taught to the children inside of that environment. It was typically come downstairs, see what's happening, and pick the most fun thing to do. Breakfast typically involved some sort of a cereal, or something that was pretty easy. Then on into the living room to watch cartoons as late as the kids were allowed.

Maybe 11:00-11:30 A.M., I would quit watching cartoons, and now it's time to eat lunch. Lunch would typically be prepared for us, five kids on a pretty modest income. Hot dogs and mac & cheese were a staple in our home. We would go outside to play for the afternoon. We had a little above ground pool in our backyard, and a fenced in area. We all had bicycles, and so riding bikes was a big past time. Often I would spend my time jumping on my bike and going for a ride.

Life was mindless. There was no thought process to why or what was happening around us. It was whimsical. What do I want to do next? Where do I want to go next? What's the next thing that I want to do? It was all based around this, whatever is whatever, concept. Throughout my day I would just bounce from one to the next to the next to the next. Typically, by about 6 o'clock at night, I would have climbed trees, ridden bikes, played with my brothers and sisters, and naturally gotten in some sort of trouble almost every day.

There just was not much structure. When I was asked to sit down and fall into a structured place, I was fidgety. You've trained me that in this environment, I don't have to do anything in any type of an order until you decide, as a parent, that you want something done.

I want you to sit down. I want you to be quiet. I want you to eat. I want you to do this, or I want you to do that. My mother and step father's parenting style was similar to prison. Either go in the yard and play or fall into a very small confined box whimsically defined by us.

My grandfather had a different approach. Our Saturdays typically began Friday night. Grandpa, at dinner would say, "Lad, Here's what we're doing in the morning. We're going to go work the hogs. We've got a couple sows that are going to be butchered. I will wake you up between 6:00 and 6:30 in the morning."

He was wise enough to add, "When we're done choring at the hog lot, we're gonna be mowing, so we're going to load up the lawnmowers and the weed eaters. I will need your help to make sure everything has plenty of gas and oil." He always made me feel like part of the team. We had jobs to do.

Once he described the routine, he would foreshadow what we were going to go do later on that was fun. We would often swim in the ponds. Grandpa would regularly have people over to the house for get togethers. We would have some sort of a fish fry or we would find a pond bank. Fishing was a favorite pastime of my grandfather, and it evolved around one of his side hustles.

"If we're going to do all of those things tomorrow, you're going to need to be laying down in bed by about 9 o'clock." Grandpa's house and his curfew versus midnight at my home with my brothers and sisters was quite contrasting. My parents required no consistent bedtime. My parents went to bed with the final words being, "Love you kids, don't make too much noise, we're going to sleep." They probably felt that it was a privilege not telling children to go to bed. Smart, but the downside to that, was that we lost structure. Sure enough at 5:30 A.M. Grandpa would begin stirring around the house and within an hour we were on our way.

Never getting onto me, only waking me up with a gentle word, "Lad, it's time to go. Let's get ready." I would wake right up, He would head into the bathroom, and I would follow suit. We'd go, I'd brush my teeth right along next to grandpa. He would shave, and I would go through my routine. I would get dressed, and we would sit down to have breakfast which grandma had made whenever we sat at the table. No blaring radio, no obnoxious TV, no Saturday morning cartoons, but great conversations about the day to come.

"Here's what the days gonna look like," Grandpa would explain. He would describe the work that had to be done. I didn't feel as though we were working though. The way he talked about the tasks at hand made it sound like an adventure.

Grandpa actually built a bait farm. He had fifteen different ponds in approximately a thirty acre piece of ground surrounding his old barn style home. He sold different types of minnows, goldfish, and worms to other people who went fishing in the area. It was a great deal for Grandpa, because selling bait was his side hustle, at least it was one of them. He chose to open the bait farm, because we also enjoyed fishing. We spent a lot of time in that environment. Consequently, we would load up the fishing equipment preparing for a large catch, and we would spend several hours on the side of a pond fishing. More wisdom than I could ever buy was given to me on the edge of those small country ponds from my greatest role model.

At the end of the day, we would walk back into the house. Usually it would be about 6:30, 7:00, 7:30 at night, and as a family we would make dinner. Grandpa wasn't a 'wife you need to have dinner ready' kind of a guy. He was a, hey, we caught some fish. I'm going to clean them, if you want to get everything ready, we'll fry the fish together. The meal was completed by picking some vegetables out of the garden. We would cut those up, and that was dinner.

My grandma and grandpa would have thawed out some of the pork or beef out of the freezer from the farm in case the fish were not biting that day. Dinner was always a family affair. Like clockwork we would finish dinner, and out of the freezer would come a little bit of ice cream. Grandpa nearly always had his on the exact same plate, not in a bowl, on a plate. He would scoop it nearly the exact same way every single time.

Then the evening would draw to a close with playing cards, checkers, chess, or an old midwestern game called Mill. If it was a game of chance, Grandpa would inevitably say, "This is not a game of skill, this is a game of chance." Normally he would say that after he just lost! Grandpa liked to win!

This is the magnified difference between a weekend at home and a weekend at Grandpa's house. A weekend with five brothers and sisters, five different personalities pulling me in five different directions, two parents who had their own individual agendas outside of the agendas of their children pushing me in another direction. Alternatively, a weekend at Grandpa's house where the entire weekend was orchestrated and executed like a machine, every single time.

As a small child, the responses are similar to the symptoms and responses of a rat in a caged medical study. The responses are magnified. Most people never recognize the power of routine, and what it has as an impact on their lives. There is a percentage of the population that recognizes that routine dictates success, and that is an advantage of the rich.

The rich recognize the power of giving their children routines. They recognize the power of having a routine themselves. They recognize that their routine isn't just a routine of bliss, a lot of times they'll put things in the routines that are intentionally hard. Rich people do things that are uncomfortable, and that they don't want to do. Through the rest of this chapter, I'm going to share with you my routine. Because I, like most people in my situation in life, have built a routine that puts me in as much power as I possibly can. The idea is that whenever I step into my day, I'm equipped to crush it! Instead of the alternative, instead of whimsically caving to the internal weak voice in your mind that says, "Oh, I want to do this, and now I want to do that, and ooh, that looks like fun."

It's time to ask yourself, "Am I like a cat swatting at a ball of yarn? Do I find myself in the position of an unprofitable day?" Get real with yourself. Be honest and reflect. Do you ever finish your day without accomplish anything?

Possibly you wake up within five minutes of the exact same time every single day. Perhaps you meditate, or you think about your day. You may even think about your accomplishments yesterday. Perchance, you think about what needs to be accomplished today. You pray; you listen for that voice inside to speak wisdom into your world. From there you might go to the gym. You go through a routine of speaking positivity over someone in your life every single day. These activities will set you up to conquer your day.

You need to get yourself to a place that allows you to succeed. You need to roll into your business, or your job, or your career, or your school, wherever your focus is in a level of power, knowing that you've accomplished more by 9 AM than most of them will accomplish all day long. You should roll out of bed before anyone else in your house. You may go to bed after everyone else in your house. To live in a place of power, your day should be systematically programmed to give you the most results.

Systematic programming is what the rich do that the poor do not. That's what grandpa understood about success in his world. He wasn't pursuing mega wealth. He was pursuing a good life, a sustainable life. A life where he never wanted for money. A life where he was able to live debt-free. A life where he could go fishing when he wanted. He could have a fish fry and have people over to his house. He could go to the local carnival, festival, or to the livestock sale, but it was what he wanted to do inside of his own terms. He did not allow his circumstances to be drug around by the world, but instead architecting the perfect world for him.

In the exact opposite, I watched my mother, her husband, as well as nearly every brother and sister that was raised inside of that house, flail aimlessly. Their goals were shortsighted. "Can we afford this?" was a common question. It was 'If this, then that' living. If I can afford this payment, then we can have that car. If I can afford that on a credit card, then we can have that pool. We want to build a deck, so they navigate a way to do that with short term results. They might take the last little bit of disposable income that they had this month, and go buy the materials to put a deck in the backyard.

Often my home life would run out of groceries the last few days of the month. We were told that we were just gonna have to get by with what was in the cupboard. On the first of the month we would start all over again. It wasn't because they were bad people, rather it was they didn't understand the power of the routine. That's how my grandpa was able to show me how to win. The win was found inside of the routine. The night before he made me go to sleep, he told me what the plan was for the next day.

He planted that little bit of a seed in advance, thus tomorrow he wouldn't have to convince me. It was a fact, this is what's going to happen today. Was there downtime? Sure, was it beneficial? Of course, I was a boy. I would go get lost in the woods for a couple of hours almost every weekend. I enjoyed climbing trees, throwing rocks, getting muddy, that's what boys do, at least that's what I did. The thing is, I didn't go do that until the work was done.

I operate that exact same way in my life today. I do wake up at 5:30 A.M. every single day. I am in a gym working out by 6 A.M. I do take time to mindfully think about my yesterday and my today. I do try to do something for the girls that I love. My wife and my two daughters are important to me, so every single day I do something for each one of them to make them feel loved. Furthermore, I try to do it before 10 A.M.

I go into work with an expectation of certain benchmarks being met. Additionally, the company that I'm building at the time can scale at a rate that's quicker than most can understand or comprehend. Living inside of a retail environment during the writing of this book, we're currently scaling a car dealership. There are some outside influences. Sometimes customer's requests and demands do pull on my time. As soon as I'm pulled away from my schedule, I address the issue, the problem, the concern, or the customer. Promptly when I'm done with that interruption, I fall right back into the preset strategy that I had for my day. The architecting of my day is essential for my success.

At the end of the day when I've completed the lists and I'm done, I shut it off and I go home. Although some nights I might not get home until 7 or 8 o'clock at night, the last few hours of my day are solely 100% focused on my family. As much attention and focus as I put into my business and into my skill, in my routine, that three hour block every single day is undivided attention from me to my family. Do we watch TV? Sometimes. Do we play games? Sometimes. Do we go to dinner? Yes sometimes but inside of that evening they get the best version of me.

At the end of each day I'm preparing for my next day, I begin planning. The very first thing that I do, this is just me personally, I check the website to see what the CrossFit workout for the next day is going to be. I plan what I need to take to the gym with me to best prepare me for that workout. I decide what I need to take as a supplement and a pre-workout.

I set those items out and get them ready for morning. Then I lay down and close my eyes. My last thought every single day is "Thank you God for today and what I accomplished. Now what am I going to accomplish in my world tomorrow?" This is every day, Monday, Tuesday, Wednesday, Thursday, Friday, and Saturday. Sunday has its own structure, but Sunday has a structured routine as well.

When you surround yourself with people who have accomplished anything in this world that they seek, you will notice routines. If you spend time with people who have any level of success or wealth, you will find that somewhere in their world is a very structured DNA'd approach to growing that vision that rests in their mind. You will also learn that more than likely their approach has been committed to paper as well. Allow that strategic planning to infiltrate your world. Personally, if you're interested in scaling your world one of the very first and most powerful things you can do is build a routine similar to what the rich build. Build a routine that circles around productivity and accomplishment.

Intrapreneurs, you work for someone else inside of their business, this applies to you as well. Your position is the business of you. You have a set number of job responsibilities, and your responsibility is to do those better than anyone else in your position. To exceed the expectations of your employer is your main objective. By doing that you will ensure that you can reap the greatest rewards. That reward might be advancement, a future partnership, additional pay, flexibility in your hours, whatever growth is important to you. Before you worry about a side hustle, before you worry about scale, before you worry about growing and doing anything extra, build a structure that supports your kingdom today.

Once you've got a systematic routine locked down, you are set up for success. Most jobs end somewhere between 4 and 6 o'clock in the afternoon. That leaves so much time for you to build the kingdom of you. Many careers don't require you to be at the office until 7, 8, 9 o'clock in the morning. That means that you could theoretically go to bed at 9 o'clock, and be up at 4 A.M. tackling your day. That would allow you ample time to accomplish more before you roll in to work than anybody else there.

This is not typically how employees think. More often than not, this is how the rich think. We recognize that when the race is in front of us, we have an opportunity to take off before anybody else in line. We have programmed our minds to execute that. We put our feet in the blocks, and we raise up just like everyone else. We're preparing for the same run around the track that you're on, but we recognize that we don't have to wait for the gun to go off in order to get started.

We get to pick when we start sprinting! When we run, we run like our hair is on fire. You can do the exact same thing. You can get ahead in the race, but it begins with structure. Take your world today and document your actions and intentions. Do a time audit of your day, and do it five days in a row. What time did I wake up? What time did I eat? What did I eat? What did I do prior to eating? Did I work out? If I did, what did I do? How long did I work out? How long did it take me to eat? How long is my commute to work every single day? What do I do with that windshield time that I spend in the car?

Numerous people frequently think I've got a 20 minute drive to work, and I just really love listening to music. Cool, I know a lot of really successful people that spend a lot of time listening to audiobooks rather than music. The successful people that I know have the same 20 minute drive to work. However, they use that time to develop their minds. Listening to an audio book or a pod case while drive is an excellent way to download knowledge without taking up any more of your precious time.

When I get to work, what do I do you ask? Do I take 15 minutes and high-five everybody? Do I walk around telling everyone good morning and horsing around by the water cooler like everyone else? Or do I go in and sit down and start grinding? Do I show up before my managers arrive? Do they wonder, man, what would I have to do to beat that guy to work? Does the ownership of the business or senior management recognize you as a leader inside of your position?

Do the employees that already work for you, if you're an entrepreneur, do they see you as the leader? Do they wonder how you get such big things done week after week, month after month, year after year? Maybe you are struggling and you drag yourself into the process that you worked your butt off to build early on in your business. Now are you at a point where you don't worry about improving? You just exist without any new effort.

Do your employees secretly hate that you make money without ever evolving the business, without ever challenging them or pushing them? In this time audit, the purpose is to evaluate where you are, and what you do with the one equally distributed commodity that we all have in this world. Time is so commonly misused and blamed in the world of business. It is your choice to reorganize the 24 hours that you are given each day to build success. Accept where you are currently. Then structure that commodity of time to put you in supreme power, and execute your butt off. Savvy?

Your Gifting

I hope you have had an opportunity to listen to my podcast by the time you are reading this. My podcast is called Bulletproof Mafia. Often on my show, I will reference something that I'm extremely good at. I will call that gift, whatever it is, my super power. It would be easy to think, wow this guy is really proud of himself. In all actuality, I am just extremely self aware. It doesn't do any good to tell you all of the things that don't create power in my life. Therefore, I continue to focus on the super powers in my life that elevate me to the next level.

For me, I have a couple of what I would consider my super powers. One of those is the ability to communicate strategically. I recognize that a good conversation or negotiation is like a dance. Inside of that skill set, not to toot my own horn, I'm a beautiful dancer. I recognize where I want to be at the end of the dance, and I lead the conversation to that point 99 times out of 100. Time and time again conversations happen exactly the way that I thought that the conversation would go in my mind. While our hands are locked at the initial greeting I am already anticipating the different directions my partner might try to take the conversation. I am mentally navigating at least three different potential outcomes all while seeking a universal path that leads to MY destination.

Another super power that I would say that I have is the ability to see potential in companies. In several instances I've bought companies that were dwindling, failing, or just not having a lot of success. I have went in and realized their potential. I have restructured processes, moved to different locations, scaled the companies, and then sold the business while it was producing.

Inside of my own businesses that I start from scratch and grow, I would say that the power to implement initial processes and building strong teams that circle around a very specific culture would be another super power of mine. I enjoy empowering teams to embrace routines and processes. Creating team culture, vision, and specific routines are what lead a company from the very early stages.

Similar to any superhero, I also didn't wake up with those skills. You know, one of the things that's really fascinating is that most all superheroes had some sort of tragedy or life event that bestowed the power upon them. Just beyond the turmoil in the superheroes life was the super power. Pushing through daily routines and processes that are effective will eventually prove to be successful.

One of the things that you're going to have to do for all of this to make any sense and be applicable to your world is have a willingness to go through the motions and trust the process that I'm mapping out for you. Inside of the chapters that we've already covered and the future chapters that are unread, I'll map out for you an action plan. I will help you plan what to do, how to think, and how to communicate in a way that will ultimately stack the deck in your favor. This preplanning will prepare you to be able to scale to wealth, wealth creation, or at least just abundance, if that's your hunt.

If you're not interested in being super rich, but you don't want to worry about how your next bills are going to be paid, then keep reading. You will be required to obtain the willingness to trust the process that I've mapped out for you. You will have to have the capacity to follow through and do those processes day in and day out, week in and week out, month in and month out, year, over year, over year, because it's not an overnight success. Daily commitment to following a plan is essential.

However, this chapter is a little bit different, because we're not talking about the structure or the mindset. This chapter is focused on super powers. This will challenge you to do an assessment of your gifts and skillsets. You're going to have to figure out what is it that you are good at. What is it that you are passionate about? What is it in your world that you can do better than most around you, no matter how obscure it might be? What can you do that adds value to the marketplace?

There is a video that I love, and I'm going to put a link to it here in the text. Also, I'm going to go ahead and just drop the entire script in the next chapter. So, this context was Steve Harvey at the end of one of his shows. Steve has talked about all these different gifts that people have. I love this, because I couldn't have said that any better. Steve's fire and passion for the success of people here is so brilliant!

https://youtu.be/QSSMsTaJiZ0

Jump

"I'm going to share something with you. I'm going to tell you something that every successful person has to do, including you.

"Believe it or not, every successful person in this world has jumped. I'm going to tell you what I mean by that.

"You eventually, you are going to have to jump. You cannot just exist in this life. You have got to try to live. If you are waking up thinking that there has got to be more to life than it is, man, believe that it is. Believe in your heart of hearts that it is, but to get to that life, you are going to have to jump.

"Now, I'll tell you why I call it jumping. See God, when He created all of us, He gave every last one of us a gift at birth. He never created a soul without endowing them with a gift.

"You just got to quit looking at gifts as running, jumping, singing, dance. It's more than that. It's if you know how to network, if you can connect dots, if you draw, you teach – some of you all fry chicken better than anyone else – bake pie. Some of you cut hair, color hair. Some people do grass trimming.

"I've got a partner, man, never wanted to go out with us because we stayed out too late. 'Come on man, go out with us. Nah, I got to get up early tomorrow. I'm cutting Ms. Johnson's grass.' We kept laughing *at this dude. 'Cutting grass, how much do they pay you?' He got a landscaping company in Cleveland worth $4 million because all he do is cut grass, but he was gifted at it.*

"I got a partner who owns a detail shop who makes $800,000 a year detailing cars. He got six mobile trucks running around. $800,000 a year, and all he do is detail cars. That's his gift. That's what he loves to do.

"You've got to identify that gift.

"Now, listen to me. When you see people in life, when you are standing on the cliff of life, and you see people soaring by and you see people soaring – going to exotic places, you hear about them doing wonderful things, maybe you look up the street and your neighbor just gets a car every year or every two years, you know how is he doing that?

"Have you ever thought, maybe this person right here has identified their gift and is living in their gift because your Bible says – this is your Bible – your gift will make room for you. Your gift. Not your education. You can go and get an education, and that's nice. But if you don't use your gift, that education is only going to take you so far. I know a lot of people that got degrees, man, they ain't even using. It's your gift.

"But the only way for you to soar is you got to jump. You got to take that gift that is packed away on your back. You got to jump off that cliff and pull that cord. That gift opens up and provides the soar.

"If you don't ever use it, you're going to just go to work. And if you getting up going to work on the job every day that you hate going to, that ain't living man. You just existing. At one point in time, you ought to see what living's like. But the only way to see what living's like, you got to jump.

"Now, here the problem. Let me just be real with you. When you first jump, let me tell you something, your parachute will not open right away. I'm sorry. I wish I could tell you that it did, but it don't. When you jump. It's not going to open right away.

"You going to hit them rocks. You going to get some skin torn off on them cliffs. You going to get all of your clothes torn off. You going to get some cuts on you. You going to be bleeding pretty bad, but eventually, eventually the parachute has to open. That is a promise of God. That ain't a theory. That's a promise.

"His promise is true because, listen to me, you cannot name one single thing God has not gotten you through. Name it. And if He ain't got you through it, He currently pulling you through it right now. And the living proof of it is, you sitting in here. If he hadn't of got you through it you wouldn't even be here.

"So, if He ain't never not got you through it, why would He not let your parachute open?

"It has to open, man. But … you got to jump though.

"Now, here's another thing. You can play it safe and deal without the cuts and the tears and you can stand on that cliff of life forever safe, but if you don't jump – I've got another promise I can make you – your parachute will never open. You will never know. You will never know what God really had for you.

"You see, your God has a wonderful life for you. Once again, I'm going to refer to your Bible. Now, you go down there. You memorize these Scriptures. You don't apply them to yourself. Your Bible says that He comes to give you life, and give you life more abundantly.

"If I were you, I would jump because that's the only way to get to that abundant life. You got to jump, man. You got to take a chance.

"Now, when I get through talking, there are those of you that will discuss this in the car, 'Well, I got bills, and I got bills." Whether you stay on the cliff or you jump, you are going to have bills. 'Well, if I quit my job I'm going to ruin my credit.' If you got a job, you living check to check. Even if you got A-1 credit, you can't buy nothing else no damn way.

"At one point in time, man, do yourself a favor. Go see what God really do. God hold you up, man. He ain't going to let you fall. He didn't bring you this far to let you fall.

"Do yourself a favor man, before you leave this world, before you die, jump. Just jump one time. Just jump. Thank you very much."

Steve talks about one thing specifically here that I think is overlooked when you watch the video. He speaks to the fact that every person has a "God given gift." You see here is the mistake that I think that most people make. Nearly all gurus, most coaches, many life advisors, they encourage you to follow in their footsteps. I'm going to show you how to make money in real estate. Look how rich I am. I'm going to show you how to make money through investing in cryptocurrencies. Look how rich I am. I'm going to show you how to get rich in the forex market. Look how rich I am. Don't be fooled.

The problem is that what they're doing after reading Steve Harvey Jump or watching the video, is they're showing you exactly their process. They might say, "Hey, I'm going to show you how I run and successfully jump off the cliff every single time. I'm going to show you how my parachute opens, that helps me land or soar safely." Unfortunately your gift set is likely different than theirs, of course there are always exceptions. If you chase the masses you will find success stories. Far too often these guys are masters at taking the few and far between success stories that they stumble on, and showcasing those like that's the norm.

Inside of my podcast, inside of this book, inside of my digital intensive training that we offer through michaelmunsterman.com, all of these things are geared towards identifying *your* gift. Identifying the chute that will open for *you*. Identifying what skill sets you have that will allow you to soar. My gifts may be different than yours, and you need your own strategic plan for success.

It will serve you to spend some time figuring out where your interest and God given gifts intersect. It is in this place that you will find the most fulfillment and normally the most profit as well. There is an alternative method, you can click through my site and work with a coach that talks you through the process of identifying your gifts and skill-sets that set you apart.

Ultimately, the goal is to figure out where your gifting lies. Regrettably, you can have all the processes, you can have all the routines, you can have the right mentality, and you can have a mind and a spirit of abundance without results. You can do everything that you need to do. You can network, have mentors, and you can educate yourself in a marketplace, all good things to prepare for success. Despite the good works, if you aren't doing that under your umbrella of gifting, then you will never reach your full potential.

The analogy of fake it until you make it is garbage. We live in a time where it's not necessary to fake it until you make it. There are kids playing video games and making $100,000 a month sharing there process of slaying everybody else in Fortnite. There are guys that love sneakers and collect sneakers that are leveraging that love for a consumer good, all the while building six and seven figure annual incomes. You are not required or expected to fake it. There is no reason for it. You are blessed with specific super powers that will enhance your ability to succeed. You must tap into those gifts and use the to their full potential.

Like Steve mentioned in his video, there are bakers who live an abundant life. Those bakers are living in abundance, because they have stepped into the marketplace and started operating inside of their gifting. They recognize that their value isn't defined by somebody telling them what they're worth an hour. Instead, their value is defined by the impact they can make in the market. How? Simply, they operate in their gift.

One of my favorite books in the entire Bible is Psalms. Inside of this phenomenal book, one of the Psalms say, your gift will make room for you! Steve Harvey mentions it again in that video. It is one of the reasons why I love that video today.

Lets expand on that just a little bit, and really zero in on what is your gift? There is a question you have to ask yourself when you're seeking to find your gift. You have to ask yourself, "What is my passion?"

For me, my passion is helping small and mid-size entrepreneurs reach their full potential. My passion is filling in gaps, sharing knowledge, wisdom, and experiences to help people scale their companies and crush their competition. My passion is to encourage young people or older people who have never had the courage to take that leap and trust in their gifts. My passion lies in giving people the ability to trust in their wings to open, and then to soar. That is my passion. Everything that I do builds up to, on top of, and around my passion.

Writing is not a passion of mine. I would never want to just sit at a desk overlooking a picturesque view, typing away insistently, hoping that somebody is going to love my literary work. To a point that if they didn't, I would be okay. Oh well, I guess it's okay they didn't like it. Book writing not my passion. However, I am writing this book for you.

So, why am I writing a book? I'm writing a book because I feel like this information that I'm sharing with you hasn't been put into a format like this. I do not believe this message has been delivered in a way that is truly applicable. I feel like everyone keeps their best information in their back pocket, and only gives you enough to try to sell you some kind of a system or program that gives them a bigger upside. I think that's unfair. Accordingly, I wrote the book to give you as much information as I possibly can to make you successful.

Why do I do a podcast you might ask? Herein lies one of my passions. I love to speak and communicate. I love to speak to people. I love to speak to and help people in and around the subjects of business, team building, process building, and scale. Communicating information that is beneficial to others and will exemplify their life is very fulfilling to me.

It just so happens that my life foundationally has a lot of tragedy. Therefore, one of the things that I would consider to be my super power is how to mitigate and overcome tragedy triumphantly on the other side. I learned to use that pain as fuel, instead of it being a dampener to my success. Tests and trials are all too familiar in my life. Instead of allowing them to dictate my future, I have allowed them to propel me to another level.

This is what you can do in your world when you recognize your super powers. Once you realize what it is that you're great at and once you realize what it is you're passionate about, you will find that those two subjects are laying right beside one another. When you pick both of them up, the rest of the journey gets much easier, because you'll discover that you organically know what to do to share your gifts with the world. If you don't have the capacity to recognize your gifting that is ok! That's where mentors come into play. Mentors can be the same people who, through an assessment of you, will be more than happy to tell you what they see as your gifts. Any mentor that is truly invested in you will quickly recognize your superpower. You just have to trust the people you employ to assess you. It sounds super easy. Unfortunately, it can be the hardest truth you can ask anyone to accept.

I was in sixth grade the first time someone told me that what I wanted didn't align with my gifts. The assessment seemed so simple. I sat in anticipation among my fellow students in the large band room, where we had been tasked to simply repeat a series of tones. Bum, bum, bum, bum dat, dat, dat, dum, bum, do, bop. With each person going ahead of me, I thought this is so easy! Mrs. Band teacher was definitely going to recognize the perfect enunciation and timing that I had rehearsed. I knew that she would instantly agree that she would be crazy to not let me pick up the drumsticks and be the perfect addition to her band! I just knew that I would someday be the best drummer in middle school history! As the students went before me, I repeated it in my head 'bum, bum, bum, bum dat, dat, dat, dum, bum, do, bop!' There was no chance I could be found lacking of anything. I imagined getting a letter, don't laugh it was 1993 people still got letters in the mail, from Metallica informing me that the only thing that would hold me back from making the band was the short length of my hair!

"Mr. Munsterman, Mr. Munsterman… MR. MUNSTER-MAN!" I snapped back to reality. Realizing that it was my turn, knowing I couldn't mess up, I opened my mouth, and I was off! "Bum, bum, bum, bum dat, dat, dat, duma… Oh crap, dum, doe, uh, Mrs. Band teacher could I please start again?" Her response cold and non empathetic, "No, everyone only gets one chance. Next." She later crushed my dreams of becoming the greatest drummer of all time.

Mrs. Band teacher actually didn't do a great job at mentoring me in middle school. However, she simply pointed out that I wasn't drummer material. She had an opportunity to speak life into my talents. Unfortunately, it was a missed opportunity for both of us on that day.

It's impossible to talk about having superpowers without talking about having weaknesses. It is as equally important to recognize your weaknesses as it is to recognize your strengths. You have to address and recognize your weaknesses. You have to be willing to look in the mirror and get very serious concerning areas that might need improvement or help. If you really want to scale and you want to soar with those other entrepreneurs that you see down the road, then you must address your shortcomings. Those neighbors who you think, "Man, they always have the newest car. They have such a nice house. Their kids are so well dressed. They seem like they have everything together, and I want that for my life." Before you can get there, you have to be able to leverage your gifts and build a team around you to support you in your weaknesses. Whether you think you are Superman or not, I promise you, there is a kryptonite.

In the last chapter we talked about routines. For me, a routine is simply a shield of protection between me and one of my biggest kryptonites, procrastination. Without routine, I find myself in chaos. I feel like I'm pulled and drawn a hundred different directions. I feel seemingly busy, but don't accomplish anything at the end of any day. I have tested this. I recognized that in order for me to grow and scale, I have to protect myself from that weakness. If I'm just left to myself to get up and try to remember, "Oh, I think this is what I was going to get done today." I'll inevitably end that day thinking, "I don't think I did anything." Most everyone has a tinge of this in them, it's why writing out your goals creates exponential growth. I simply recognize that in my life this desire for structure creates the best version of my life daily.

Another example of one of my kryptonites is that I am not a detailed oriented person. I'm a visionary, not an implementer. There's a really great book on this subject. It's called Rocket Fuel, and it talks about that V.I. combination. You're either a visionary, or you're an implementer. You're either the guy that has the vision and can see the future... Well, not see the future exactly, but sees into his future, and can architect something back from that. Alternatively, you could be the person that the visionary works with by saying, "Here is our vision, here's what we want to accomplish." Once they share their vision, you are that person that can build the machine that implements it moving forward. At the very least, you support the visionary through that walk and grab the little pieces that they step over or miss.

In order for me to protect myself from this particular version of my kryptonite, I have to almost always lean on my wife. In the world of our different companies, she is my implementer. When a company grows to scale, to a point that it is outside of what she wants her commitment to be, I will hire someone who has her same skill sets. Other times the industry is outside of a category of business that she's comfortable working. In those instances, I will hire an implementer from the start.

Inside of our car dealership, my daughter is the implementer. She handles 100% of the accounting, processes, controls cash flow, and all of the little necessary minute details that I would otherwise miss. I make sure that the company scales, grows, and that the marketing is on point. I ensure that customers continue to fall into that funnel. Her job is to use the machine that I created to catch the flow of sales.

I only use the examples of my business and personal strengths and weaknesses to demonstrate standards. What you have to be willing to do inside of your own role is look at where your weaknesses are. Once they are realized, you can use that to your advantage. Further you need to develop a strategy to shield yourself from those weaknesses.

Maybe you are a non-conformist who has been working for someone else your entire life. When you're told what to do, without any question from you, do you think this is a good idea? Is this something that would work based on your experience? If you're in an environment where people just say, "Do this thing. Do this thing the way that I say to do it, and do this thing right now!" Every time you're told to do something in that fashion a little bit of your soul dies. Immediately, the very first thing that you could do is switch employers. Or, recognize that maybe you're not designed to have an employer from the start. You're potentially designed to be an entrepreneur, and that will insulate you from mindless orders. For you that could create a future where you fall into a routine, leveraging your gifts for the marketplace, without being told what to do. Instead, being driven because of the value that you add to the market.

I have met people that have a different weakness, their kryptonite is sleep. They just love to sleep. They tell me, "Oh, when I get home I am instantly tired. I just want to go to sleep." Their entire life suffers because instead of going to bed at a decent time they stay up late watching TV or playing on their phones.

Only going to sleep when they have completely drained their energy reserves. This normally only works for young people.

Almost inevitably, the thing that's holding them back from the best version of their life is the lack of structure in their world. There is plenty of time to get eight or nine hours of sleep in a day and still have an incredibly successful life. The shielding for that is that they're going to have to cancel their Netflix subscription. Go to bed at a decent predetermined time. For example, the same time that they put their children to bed. Structure is obtainable, but it requires effort.

There are a million example just like this. Examples where you can look into your own world and recognize your giftings, recognize your weaknesses, recognize your super power, or recognize your kryptonite. Leverage and wearing your super powers, or your giftings, on your chest like a badge of honor is critical. Mindfully shielding yourself from the kryptonites that could potentially hold you back. You must block those weaknesses that could potentially hold your gift back from the world. Savvy?

It's Your Movie

Savvy is designed to change the way you think! It's designed to inspire you to believe that you can, regardless of where you come from, crush whatever dreams and desires you currently have! Before you can be successful in any area of your life, you first have to be able to defeat that little "weak version of yourself" that is constantly talking and complaining in the back of your mind. Controlling and testing yourself physically is the first step to directing your life mentally.

When I'm consulting with startup companies or single industry generational companies I'm typically asked the same few questions listed below:

1. How do you know how to proceed as you venture into a new business or new industry?

2. We started a company. We've got the company running. We sourced our products. We rented a space. We even hired an attorney to get ourselves an LLC. We got everything rolling. Now how do we scale our current business from where we are to where we aspire to be?

3. Everything was going great but we have had some stuff come up and our business feels like it is spiraling out of control! How do we guide the ship?

Starting a company, scaling a company, or getting an existing company that is broken back on track is no different than writing a good movie script. You start with an idea of how it ends and then you architect your storyline, sets, props, and talent. Your job is to direct that movie while keeping that end scene in mind. Now, I'm not a director. I am not a producer. I'm not even an actor. I understand how to write and build beautifully crafted business models that are executable and typically, more often than not, have a happy ending for myself and my investors. Savvy?

The Power of Paper

Ideas are just ideas until they are committed to paper. Once written down that idea becomes a goal. Essentially, goals aren't any different. First you need to commit your "ideas" to paper. I typically start with an outline that touches the highlight reel of what I am trying to accomplish. Don't worry so much about the little details. They will come to you as you refine your goals. I always verbalize exactly what I want out of an opportunity and what I think it can look like. The human mind is so brilliant! Your mind can tell you what your business will look like if you will simply follow the steps that you get from the voice inside of you.

God, the universe, whatever your belief system, will guide you. For me, it's God that illuminates my path. I believe that God gives me this innate ability to see into the future. No, not the future, like I cannot tell you what the next card is going to be at a blackjack table or what the winning lottery numbers are this week. What I can see is the future into my own life and ability to create inside of my life. If it's clear enough that I can see it in my mind's eye, it's clear enough that I can create it in this world. The most essential key for me after I visualize an idea is to write it down on paper.

Now, without getting too mumbo jumbo or head in the clouds, let me explain what I mean. If I can describe to you that in my business, I expect it to look like this, I expect it to run a certain way, I need this many employees and this is how they all work together, then we can all be driven by one common theme or goal. If I can speak it, I can script it, which means I can write it down. If you write it down correctly you can execute it flawlessly.

There are an enormous amount of experts that will tell you how essential it is to write down your goals. I completely agree with them. Essentially, they leave out the most important part, what they don't talk about is why. Why should you write down your goals? Whereas, when you write down your goals, you clarify the script. Every guru in the world starts by creating a plan with clear objectives. It's seems like the most unpractical advice in the world. Am I telling you to buy a notebook and write that you want to be rich inside? Boom! Presto! You are rich! After all, no one is going to understand why goal setting works without thorough investigation, and they are simply going to dismiss it as a good chapter in the book without taking any real action.

In order for the movie analogy to make sense we have to start by answering the most basic question. Why do I write down my goals? When you write down your goals, you can begin to visualize your end product. Writing goals will force you to visualize the idea to completion. Furthermore when you can see the end result, you will know how your movie ends. This realization will give you the ability to write the story. Knowing how your idea should look at completion helps you to navigate the perfect road map!

Now remember, for an idea to be a goal it has to three parts, just like a great movie script. First, an idea has to have a definitive final scene. This is something that is measurable and precise. The script doesn't say at the end of the famous Ghostbusters movie that the good guys win. You can't do that either. You can't just write goals that are broad. A goal stating you will get healthier does not enable you to formulate a road map. Rather, you might say that your one mile run time that is currently 11 minutes and 20 seconds will decrease to 9 minutes and 55 seconds. A goal written like that will give you a traceable, definitive finish line. Next, you have to set a time in the future that you will accomplish the task. Most movies are broken into scenes that are structured around budgets and timelines based on the storyline. Using our same example your storyline would say that you are going to cut my one mile run time from 11 minutes and 20 seconds to 9 minutes and 55 seconds in the next 90 days. You almost have everything you need to get started towards your path. The very last set is to commit this to paper. Committing your goals to paper will cause you to focus and keep you on the right road map. Congratulations you can celebrate your first written goal!

This is your movie. By writing goals you now know where you are and what the final outcome will look like at completion. Straightaway you have the opportunity to write the script for your movie. Beginning to write the script of your story, as well as writing your goals, you have to be very clear which means you have to be unquestionably specific. Why do you have to be transparent? Why do you have to be precise? When writing goals you have to be clear, so that you can be specific! You have to be clear-cut. It's not enough just to write down on the piece of paper some generalized idea and think woo hoo, the job is done. It's like saying a prayer and hoping that everything just falls into place. I often tell people you can't pray from your couch and expect great results without actually getting off of your couch.

Numberless spiritual people think about it like this, all I need to do is say a prayer and expect a result. My mission will be accomplished! Well, that is not exactly how it works. They believe I'm going to pray and that's it. Unfortunately, there is often a little bit more of a requirement on your part. Prayer plus work equals results. Prayer plus actions equals results. For the sake of this conversation, you can liken prayer to having an idea in your head. Until you commit that idea to paper, it is just another great wasted idea. Are there some things that you care about and believe for that you have no ability to impact? Absolutely there are. However, we're not talking events that are out of your control. We're talking about business goals. We're talking about writing the script to your dreams and your life. We're talking about building your company. We're talking about scaling your empire to where you dream of it someday being. You say it's not good enough to be at $5,000 a month in sales, or it's not good enough to be at $10,000 a month in sales. That voice in your head will tell you to expect $24,000 a month in sales. Let's make a road map to enable you to get there! Today, however, you might be only doing $2,000 a month in sales. If you want to reach another level you will need to write the script, pave the way, create your road map to the next level.

By intentionally being very clear in your goals, you open the pathway internally to be very specific. The reason it is important to be specific is because the exact details will dictate what you do next. In writing a really great movie your first step is to build out the wire frame or the outline. In other words, you map out the general scenes working backwards from the closing scene rearwards all the way to the opening credits. For example, you have one sales person and that one person is doing $2,000 a month in sales. You feel like they have the capacity to get to $8,000 per month. To reach the goals of $24,000 in sales you will eventually need three sales people performing at an $8,000 per month rate.

Being very clear in your goals will cause you to expand and grow your business. In order to support three sales people with incoming leads, phone calls, with the paperwork you are probably going to need a receptionist. Okay that's clear. Now, let's look at another leg on here. In order to sell more products you are going to have to beef up your infrastructure in all areas: inside of manufacturing, inside of warehousing, inside of distribution, and inside of advertising. Every single leg of the very clear, very specific, written goal set now has to be orchestrated around your "end game". We have to internally dig deep and document. I'm getting this feedback internally, in my mind, now I have to take this feedback from my mind and apply it to paper.

What's happening the entire time that you are changing business levels? The story is getting more and more clear. The end result is becoming more and more evident. The final scene is becoming more and more transparent, and you can't help but begin to take the necessary steps today to make it come to fruition. As you become more clear on the end game you enable yourself to see where steps are being missed in the front game. You'll find that those missteps will drive you crazy. You are wondering if your business partners have read the script. Don't they know the story? I know how this ends.

Mastering your script is essential. Creating your storyline to fit inside of your business is essential. As your storyline becomes more and more clear, you are able to direct the ship. You're creating a wire frame, scene one, act one, scene one, act two. You have realized the number of characters that are essential to have in each scene. You're realizing their roles and what you as a director expect them to do, and then your business can begin to hire. Now again, there are some steps in there. Hiring the right employees is like a coach forming a team. They all need to work together for YOUR movie script.

I will use the same example as I did earlier. You have somebody that does $2,000 a month in sales and you believe they have the capacity to get to $8,000. That means you, as the owner of the company, have to figure out a way to provide them with enough leads to enable them to sell to $8,000. You have already established internally, in your mind, that you believe you could do $24,000. That means you have an idea of what it's going to take to make it rain.

Some questions that often arise in every business are: Well, should I get the product first? Why, you don't have the sales? Should I ramp up advertising? The answer is maybe. Is my marketing strong? Again, the answer is maybe. Could it be my social media presence? Definitely need to think about that, but that's just part of the scene. Typically all of these different little elements are going through your mind as you're looking at each individual scene. Currently, we are focusing on sales, getting from $2,000 to $8,000 for this one sales person so you can hire the next person that you envision in the scene.

You can see how strategically you can take this process of writing and really evaluating your business internally. This is what coaches do. Numerous amounts of entrepreneurs hire coaches to assist them down this internal path. Essentially, all you have do is write down your goals, right? This is where all these jokers who call themselves business coaches and leaders tell people to just write down goals. Suitably, just think about that as you're thinking why am I writing down my goals? You're making a movie. You are creating your very own movie with a specific storyline.

Now fast forward because I am not going to bore you to death with all of the crazy intricate details of this right? You've got to build the set which means the environment has to be conducive to the movie. You must have the right people in place. Like I imagine I can probably be an actor. However, I can't imagine that I could walk in and do what a Brad Pitt can do. I couldn't walk in and do what a Tom Cruise can do. These are crazy talented actors that excel at their career.

There are crazy talented actors that excel at their career. A good example that I need to share is Christian Bale and Heath Ledger. Do you know what they have in common? Other than they acted in the Batman franchise? What I love about their acting styles is that they are what's considered method actors. Which means that they shift into these different roles. You'll see them in one movie crazy buff like Bale was in Batman and then in another one when he lost 70 pounds. He had an extremely scrawny look in the Machinist. The effort that these men put into creating a role that needs to be filled to make the movie.

I couldn't do that. I have no desire to bulk up and get crazy strong just to lose it all. Often actors will shrink down to look like a homeless person who hasn't eaten in thirteen weeks and is on a thirty day drug binge. However, as entrepreneurs we have to be able to mentally switch between very dramatic roles. There has to be a willingness to dive deep into each role. Assuming the identity of that role is required until you understand the multitude of necessary nuances you will need to be as successful as that character in your story. As I'm progressing in my own movie my mind controls me going too far outside the bounds in any given role. In other words you'll need to recognize your ability to play most of the characters in your script. It is necessary however to remind yourself that unless you want to just be self employed, you will need to stay in the directors chair. Hire those brilliant people that can do the things you aren't as gifted. Maybe you can't do what they can do or sometimes you hire people because you don't want to perform the tasks expected of them.

Grandpa used to say to me, "Lad you're so busy looking at the top rung of the ladder, you can't see the rung that's right in front of your face." And I so eloquently challenged my grandfather, like I always did. I said, "Grandpa, I'm not just looking, I'm jumping at it. And if I miss it, I still land three rungs higher than the one that was right in front of my face which is where everyone else is fighting for." I was visualizing my goals, envisioning the necessary rungs on the ladder and sprinting past everyone else that wanted the same things. Eventually Grandpa saw that I had an aptitude for business and would give me advice then hear out my response. He encouraged me to write down even the most obscure thoughts. Today I have a pile of journals that contain my goals. It is always fun to look back at those and marvel at how when I map out the script the universe moves to make it happen. Early on I didn't know why it was so important to write my goals. I didn't understand the movie that was being written.

Now I understand that every time I start a company I am writing a new movie. I'm creating a production and the end game is my goal. And everything in between are the details necessary to product the movie. I'll expand on certain bits of this later, but at its core this is why you write your goals. I get that this sounds very cosmic and sort of corny. Try it. What do you have to lose? Savvy?

If You Prepare The Soil A Tree Will Grow

You now have several fundamental tools floating around that ought to give you a basic due north that is, and will continue to be, necessary as we navigate the final few sections of Savvy. By now, I would expect that you would have your why clearly defined. You should also have listed the mentors that have influenced you. You should be constructing a list of mentors that you would like to surround yourself with, books you want to read, and mentors that you could pay to help you elevate to the highest levels in your industry. You should by now understand that breaking ourselves physically gives us the ability to step out as an entrepreneur with confidence and clarity knowing that you will not allow your mind to sabotage the goals that you will set for yourself.

I am trying to till up the ground in your mind. I want Savvy to prep the soil, so that together we can plant the seeds of your gift and watch as you bear your fruit to the world. I want the roots to go so deep that when the harsh winds of reality smack against your canopy you will have the capacity to stand firm, taller than ever, and remain completely unbroken.

Before we are ready to implement the plan, it is time to crush some habits that I see in almost every person that I talk to. Lets establish a couple of truths. First and foremost the thoughts that you generate in your head are no different from fresh bread from your local bakery. They spit out of the oven of your mind long after you have dumped in the ingredients. You see, what you put in your mind will 100% dictate what your mind produces as a final produced thought.

This was a hard lesson for me to learn. At my mom's house we were conditioned to either sit in the living room and watch TV like everyone else or go play. The only inputs that were available to me were the school, radio, TV, family, or local neighborhood kids. There were no cellphones, no Google, wiki-what is that?! I've already expressed that my mother and step father didn't have the human bandwidth to invest in 5 children, work full-time jobs, and maintain their sometimes rocky relationship. Just directing traffic was a hard enough challenge for them; let alone invest in deep meaningful conversations that would teach us how to think and process like rational adults.

Grandpa's house, however, was entirely different. There was no TV. No one ever said, "Go play." Sometimes you would hear top country hits playing on an old-time radio. However, if I wanted to be entertained I was expected to pick up one of the magazines, newspapers, or books that were laying around the house. Grandpa's house gave me the opportunity to focus on a global perspective of what was happening in the world.

I was always very fascinated with Grandpa's ability to discuss current events. His knowledge base seemed to dwarf anyone else I had ever met. The truth is, he didn't waste time filling his head with garbage. He filled his mind with intelligent media only. When he would step out of grind mode, he was a brilliant communicator who was versed in most all of the current events. I know he didn't invent the phrase, "Readers are Leaders", but he was the first person to ever say it to me. He recognized that our minds were mixing bowls. What we put in determined what we would get out.

Now we live in a world where media is literally attached to our hands. Where you never have to wonder, about anything! You can try to imagine the absolute most absurd nonsense ever and you will likely find a multitude of extensive content that supports it. YouTube videos show talking fruit. Television shows that have been broken up and scattered across our social landscape, mountains and mountains of digital garbage are ready for human brain consumption. The sad part is that most people can't consume it quick enough!

You have to decide if you are committed to not only filling your mind with the correct ingredients, but also ensuring that you follow the cooking times and temperatures to a tee if you plan on successfully preparing your mind for wealth. This will prepare you for success. When the things that come from you are produced for the world, they actually taste good! The world will want what you have been creating with your thoughts.

Consequently why do I have to worry about what I watch? What I read? What I discuss? What I allow myself to think about? Who I surround myself with? What I do in my free time? What I allow others to say to me? And mostly what I say about myself?! Every input and output that is created around us, or from us, leaves a trace inside of the neurons of our mind.

Grandpa and I would sometimes drive through the different fields around the farm. He had established acceptable paths that we were supposed to stay on in order that we wouldn't hurt the planted crops. I was around eleven the first time he let me drive the old Chevy truck around the farm without him. As soon as I was over the hill and out of sight, I began to think that I could save some time by cutting across the field instead of following the given path grandpa had created. I remember it so vividly, because I didn't realize that everywhere I drove in the field would leave a trail. Our minds are no different, even though you go through it pretty quickly, it leaves traces of you having been there. If you do it one time there is a chance that it could recover and fill in most of the gaps. In time you might not even be able to tell that you had veered off the path. Accordingly, what happens when you back up over the same spot or you drive over that same path multiple times? A distinct path is created. One that impacts the productivity of that crop all the way through to the harvest. You can imagine how surprised I was when grandpa asked me if I had stayed on the path! I quick thought, "Did he see me or did I leave a trail?" Either way I couldn't lie to my grandpa, so I just told him the truth. Grandpa explained to me that just like the hay, the places we go and the things we do leave tracks. We have to make sure that we use that information to our advantage.

I don't pretend to understand how the mind works in relation to the results in our life. However, I can just tell you that everything that I have been building in my life would be pointless if I didn't have the correct mindset. One of the things I have spent hundreds of hours studying is the human mind. How it consciously and sub-consciously responds to the cues presented to it in our everyday lives is intriguing. This skill has allowed me to train my mind for success. I have also learned how the environments and word tracks we create in our companies create a safe place with controlled stimuli for our customers. Environments where specific cues are created with the intent of moving our customers and potential partners to a place where they are more easily influenced. I could write an entire book on this one principle. For the sake of this conversation, I want to focus on how we can support our mind's capacity to allow scale and growth in your life.

You have to recognize that everything you experience leaves a trace in your mind. This means that everything you see, everything you learn, every conversation you have, and everything you confirm with your mouth creates connections between the neurons in your brain. This alters the way you think FOREVER! This information is invaluable! You must invest in yourself and in what goes into your mind.

Some of the thoughts you have are short term; some of them are long term. The more travelled thoughts and the ones that are mixed with higher intense emotions, generally speaking, are stored in the long term part of our brain. Our long term memory will affect how we handle short term situations almost always. Short term memories are like firecrackers. They leave little bits of debris in our minds and a slight ringing in our ears; however all of that fades away pretty quickly.

It has taken a lot of time for me to specifically stomp down the trails that allowed me to learn communication techniques for the different people in my life. The hardest person I have ever tried to master my intellectual sparring with, believe it or not, is…me.

Let me set the stage for the rest of this chapter. Inside of your mind there are two versions of you. They are simply Positive You and Negative You. One of them needs positivity and value based input. While the other requires negativity and fear to survive. Imagine them with me, the day you were born there were two newborns in your mind. At five years old there were two separate five year olds in your mind. By the time you were 18 there are two fully developed conscious beings standing side by side in your mind. They constantly are listening to you and then giving you feedback. One of them stands in the lime light of your thoughts and one of them looms in the shadows. One has absorbed absolutely every positive thought you have had, book you have read or encouragement you have received, and now gives those thoughts to you. The other has absorbed the scoldings, the fear, the negativity and gives that back ten fold.

If we asked ten different people which version stands in the light based on what I wrote in the preceding paragraph, the assumption would be the Positive You stands in the light while the Negative You cowards in the shadows. Unfortunately, if that was your guess more often than not, you would be wrong. For most people, the light in their mind is directed towards negativity, albeit masterfully masked inside of "what is best for you."

From the time most small children are old enough to understand, they would be told to conform to what has long ago been established as how children ought to act and be parented. For most of us it was a generationally repeated rhetoric that wasn't necessarily the best advice. Instead we received a regurgitated parenting style echoed from our grandparents through our parents and into us. The exact same things that were said to them for "their own good" are now being given to young people as good sound parenting advice:

1.   That will never work.

2.   Better to be safe than to be sorry.

3.   Be quiet, sit down.

4.   You're too young to understand.

5.   Hush.

6.   Don't make me tell you again.

7.   Stop that.

8.   How many times have I told you not to do these stupid things?

As you read these eight common phrases spoken to children, the thing that you should notice about all of them is that they have a negative connotation. Remember, the light version of you can't absorb this content. Your parents inadvertently fed the Negative One within you. Even worse, some of us were threatened physically, emotionally beat down, and abused. Every negative input acting like a steroid shot to the darker version of you. More often than not, if you could see into the minds of the average eighteen year old kid you would see a visible difference between the size and confidence of the Negative One living inside of them. By the time these same young people are thirty or thirty five the positive version is nearly gone altogether. Most people don't even realize how broken they are due to their own thinking.

Grandpa had a different approach. Listen to how he would communicate with me, saying a variation of the above negative sentences:

1. When you try that, what do you think will happen?

2. You will never know unless you try.

3. Lad, act more level headed.

4. Walk with your eyes open, Savvy?

5. I want to hear what you think about this, when it's your time to talk.

6. Lad, remember why that wasn't the best choice?

7. Take it easy.

Did you notice that there is not a number eight? That is because I don't remember a time ever that I was attacked directly. All influence stemmed from a loving, positive place. He spoke without games, without negotiations, and without negativity. Instead he spoke with compassion and an understanding of his audience: a young, shattered boy who had lost his father and his best friend. My grandpa just loved me.

Take the analogy simply as the way I am describing it. I am not suggesting that these people are bad or that the negative inner person represents evil. I am simply saying that a lifetime of comments like the following have drowned out many hopes and dreams:

- Rich people are greedy.

- Rich people have figured out a way to add value to the world.

- Money is the root of all evil.

- Money is a measurement for the value you give the world.

- Have not want not.

- You can accomplish anything you put your mind to.

- You will never be rich.

- What are you passionate about?

- Money doesn't grow on trees.

- If you want that, we should create a plan for you to save up enough money.

- We can't afford it.

- This is something we will have to save up to purchase.

- We will never have that.

- You can have anything you want if you are willing to work for it.

- We could never afford that.

- Everyday we are working to better ourselves. That is something that I am excited to be able to buy.

I'm spending a considerable amount of time showing you how most people's minds are programmed. Even if they were given a million dollars they would squander it quickly. Because the necessary version of their inner person hasn't been fed, it hasn't been worked out. In fact for most, it hasn't been relied on in a really long time.

Many people are now masked with a "this is the hand I was dealt" mentality. Even though they look happy, they just aren't. Numerous good people are conditioned like dogs, to sit, to stay, and some sadly enough to even beg.

You see there is a competitive edge when you understand the way the mind works. You have the opportunity to control everything in your world, and it all starts with eyes and ears. It is time to filter what you allow into your world. This has to happen in conjunction with the mechanics of obtaining wealth. Your mind will need to be sharpened, and the positive version of you needs to be fed. It needs to be exercised. It needs to be challenged. It has to be stronger than ever. You simultaneously and intentionally have to beat down the negative you. Being an entrepreneur is not fun and games. It is hard work. It will test your commitment and your stamina. The positive you will have to be stronger than it has ever been, and it will need a very clear picture of your why seared into it's minds-eye.

As you begin to exercise the control you have internally, everything that enters your mind will have to be filtered through this question, "Is this a positive or a negative input?" If it is a negative and you have the ability to avoid or delete it, you absolutely should. If it is positive, don't just let it slip through. Take time to truly absorb it. Positive input needs to be savored.

Now the hard part, in the beginning of this practice when you originate thoughts you have to remember, there are two voices fighting for the microphone. It will not always be easy, but you must remain consistent. You have to be willing to not allow the negative to speak into your world. In time that version will become starved for attention. It will get weaker as you mindfully condition yourself to not allow it a voice in your mind any longer. Before you know it, your life will absolutely shift. You will see a new level of abundance. Positivity will drive your workouts, your goals, your days, your months, and your entire life. People will likely recognize a new version of you. That is when the fun truly begins. Savvy?

Let Them Work For You

As I have grown older I realize that the things that made me the most money were legal and typically involve not doing the same things everyone else does. Like I had mentioned previously, Grandpa had said to me, "Lad, you have to learn to walk with your eyes open, savvy?!" I learned to recognize the patterns of commerce. I watch the masses to see which way they are moving. I have learned to make it a habit to look the opposite way and see what they are missing or leaving unattended.

Countless people wake up every day, drink their coffee, eat their breakfast and head off to work. They do this over and over and over again. Never stopping to ask themselves, "What if ten or fifteen people woke up everyday and came to work for me?" What will your life look like when you decide to leverage the talents of others for your cause? Just think of the potential impact you could make on society.

You might be thinking I couldn't do that; I don't know what I am doing. Maybe you are thinking, "Man I wish I would have went to/ or completed college! Then I would know exactly how to change my life." There is nothing magical about the piece of paper you receive at the end of four years of university. You simply need to commit to the process of incremental adjustments daily that will improve your life over time.

The truth is that I shudder every time a young person tells me they are going to college unsure of what they want to do on the other side of that decision. I want to rip them from the mold that they are being shoved through. Instead I want to show them that if they would have faith in their gifts and walk with their eyes open, that soon they would be in the elite three percent. Unfortunately, its not my place to stop them. The few times I have had one of those conversations with younger people about college, their parents are pretty quick to encourage them to "do the right thing." The safe thing is promoted by the parents. The smart thing is what most parents desire for their children. Parents encourage their children to go spend $100,000 on a degree that the teenagers are unsure of what the heck they plan to do as a career goal.

I suggest that everyone read Robert Kiyosaki's book, **Rich Dad Poor Dad**. Robert does a great job of describing the difference between the small percentage of our society that constitutes the rich versus the masses of our population. The difference between the ones that use money and the ones who are trapped by it. Savvy?

$100,000 Journey To What?

College can be a great life path. I especially believe this if you know what you want to do, where you want to go, and have the support system to ensure that you stay between the lines. If you go to college because that is the next step, then I have a better idea. Jump on Instagram find me, @michaelmunsterman. I will sell you practical real business advice for the same $100,000! Obviously I am joking, well sort of.

What does college have to do with what I'm talking about? Let me explain. I have two daughters, one of them is 25 and the youngest is a 18 year old senior in high school. My oldest daughter went to college and graduated in a little over 3 years. She recognized that in order for college to make sense she needed to get through it as quickly as possible. She knew that she would need to get a degree in something that she could leverage in the marketplace. My oldest daughter chose accounting, and now she handles the finances of our different companies. She is extremely accomplished and continues to impress me every single day! Could she have got to the same place without a degree? I'm not sure, maybe. What I can tell you is that her experience has added a much needed implementation viewpoint to offset my visionary perspective.

My youngest daughter has showed interest in several different fields but is currently feeling called to be a speech pathologist. She has decided that if she is going to spend four to six years in college, she expects to be compensated accordingly. What I love about her logic is this; she isn't going to college to get paid. Her first concern is the value and impact that she can add to the world. However, she is grounded enough to recognize that a $200,000 piece of paper should equate to a much larger multiple for her efforts. Having graduated with an unweighted 4.0 GPA she was able to secure a full-ride scholorship to the university of her choice. Her path allows for vast employment opportunities as well as entrepreneurial ventures in a field that will never run out of need. Whether we pay for their degrees or not, I expect my girls to understand the expense of institutional education.

College has it's place. So many graduates exit university with a plethora of new skills that better enable them for the grueling, "real world." If you are going to send your children to university or go back to school yourself, make sure there is a very specific and clear plan of use for that education.

If you are going to step out of the "Rat Race", as Robert Kiyosaki calls it in Rich Dad Poor Dad, then you will have to learn to rise above the years of forced conformity and remember who you are at your core. You are a brilliant gifted human being who is currently somewhere in the middle of your one chance to crush this life. Break the mold and go for it! Regardless of what "it" is in your life.

If you can begin to recognize the patterns of conformity then you will begin to organically reject them. You will stop accepting the matrix that we have all been placed. Remember in the movie, "The Matrix", Morpheus gives Neo the choice to take the blue pill and be returned back to his life, agreeing to accept everything the way he understood it prior to being told the truth. However, the red pill is described as the solution for knowing the real truth in life. He tells Neo that he can advance into the "rabbit hole" or in other words, continue to learn about the lies that were set in the world in order to break them and obtain freedom.

You will begin to see that the world is your oyster. Your ability to live the very best version of the life of you is there for the taking. Savvy?

I'm Not Your Voice

Earlier in the book I talked about physicality and working through physicality not simply for the vanity of physicality, but rather to strengthen who you are as an individual person. Strengthen that voice that supports and gives encouragement, that voice that speaks up when you're traveling down the right path, or when it's time to pick a different course of action. That small voice that, when you were little, screamed inside of your head so loud, "This is what we want. This is what we're going to accomplish. This is where we're going to go," and you just listened to it. You must become childlike again and trust that voice inside of you.

Through years of being told no, being oppressed, being pushed backwards and getting pushed back that voice has taken some terrible setbacks. When you would make comments like, "When I grow up I wanna be rich," that voice got weaker and weaker and weaker. You began to listen to the negative voice in your head, the one that says things like, "You can't do that. That will never work. What will so-and-so think? How will you ever show your face at the golf course after you do that? What will Mom think? What will Dad think? What will my brothers and sisters think? What will my wife think? What will my kids think? You're gonna be so embarrassed when you fail." That negative voice inside of you has been allowed to grow and echo inside of your head. You have given that voice so much power throughout the course of your life. You have given that voice the ability to speak into and alter your course. Thereby the negativity has altered your reality and prevented your reality from positively impacting others to its maximum capacity.

Hopefully, as you've progressed through this book you've seen that I have been able to overcome that voice. In my story on the other side of tragedy, a lack of physicality, on the other side of lots of hurdles and obstacles in my lifetime, I've figured out how to strengthen that positive voice that said, "We can do this." I put myself in front of the appropriate mentors that reinforced the positivity in my head. I surrounded myself with guys that would challenge me if what I was saying didn't align with my goals. They had the power and the wisdom to out loud speak life into my world. These mentors would reinforce that spoken word with positivity. They taught me that if I wanted to excel, I not only had to strengthen that voice, but I also had to listen to it.

It starts small. It's the voice that, at 5 A.M., says, "It is time to get up." Recognizing that it's the negative voice that you've been listening to for the last decade of your life that says, "Five more minutes, hit snooze." Listen to the voice that will enhance your success.

It's the voice that says, "One more round, one more rep, push a little bit harder." I get it you have been yo-yoing back and forth. You've been listening to the voice that says, "Oh, we're tired, let's just stop." Quiet the negative voice in your head.

It's the voice that says, "You're not quite done with your day. Thirty more minutes, and you'll get accomplish everything that you set out to accomplish today." Regrettably, you've been listening to the voice that says, "My favorite TV show comes on tonight, it's time to go right now." That negative voice will get quieter as you begin to ignore it.

It's the voice that says, "Before you turn on the TV, talk to your spouse about their day. Ask your kids what their day was like." Unsuccessfully, you have been listening to the voice that says, "I'll do that later." Shut down the voice that is causing strain on your most important relationships.

You have given so much power to the negative voice in your head that most days you barely hear the stronger, positive voice. Consequently, through working out and challenging yourself physically, you have an opportunity to strengthen that voice. Every single day you get to set a bar in front of it that allows you to blast through and strengthen that voice. When the alarm goes off and it's time to get up, your decision to follow that voice's prompting gives it strength inside of you. Every time you follow the prompting of the positive voice in your mind, you strengthen it.

Your decision to get up, your decision to grind just a little bit harder, your decision to make those calls that you don't wanna make at work, your decision to call those leads, reach out to that prospect, do the marketing, all of the things that you need to succeed are being whispered inside of your head. You just have to make the decision to listen, and every single time that you do it gets a little bit stronger. That is one more repetition, that's one more reinforcing action to the positive prompting in your mind. Soon that voice will drown out the negative voice to a small whisper.

It doesn't take nearly as long to strengthen that voice as it does to smother it. This isn't a lifetime of work that you've got ahead of you. This is Ninety days of allowing the positive voice to be heard. Inside of Ninety days of making a conscious decision, making a list of the areas that you're the weakest, making a list of the areas that you're coming up short, making a list of the areas that you wanna see markable improvement, making a list of the things that you need to do every single day to live your best life, and then listening to that voice and make the decision to act. To follow that prompting. Ninety days is not forever. You can do this.

I've talked to you in this book about getting your mind right. I have discussed the creative and mental paths that we make when we allow our mind to work one way or another. I explained to you that the more you travel over a path the more defined and visible it is for you. What I didn't tell you is that there is a GPS inside of your mind that will take you wherever you set the destination.

I talked to you about visualizing your goals, writing those goals out in very specific details, and breaking them back into actionable steps. The smartest influencer in your world is the one that has the absolute most data points about you, about your life, about your circumstances, about your opportunity, about your path. It's you. It has been you all along. You just have to make the decision to say yes. You have to make a conscious decision to listen to the voice. To feed it, to follow it, and to execute your butt off.

The biggest challenge you will have is in the first thirty days. You will be challenged, because that other voice is going to squeal. The negative voice inside of your own mind is going to fight you. You are mentally going to ... be sabotaged. You will have a physical manifestation of negative emotion, aches, and pains that don't make any sense. You will believe that you can't continue. You will believe that you don't have any more gas in the tank. You will believe that those key relationships that you are trying to save can't be saved.

That voice is gonna pull out every single stop to derail you from smothering him and putting him back in the corner of your mind where it belongs. That negative voice, it never goes completely silent. Henceforth, the voice inside of you that will rule will be the voice that you feed, the voice that you follow, and the voice that you put the work in behind and support. Make the choice to follow the voice that will make your life flourish.

Your best life is on the other side of the decision to do what you already know you should be doing. You are reading this book because that voice was in you your entire life. That voice is still in you right now, and it's holding onto an image of wealth and prosperity that's being flung in front of it online. It is saying to you, "This should be us. We want to be rich." You just have to make the decision to execute your giftings, to do the work, and to listen to that voice. By doing so, your life will forever be changed. Ninety days from now it will be unrecognizable to those around you! Savvy?

Savvy?

I believe that every single person who has read this book is destined to impact the life of at least one other person. For many of you, your ability to create change and live the life that you've always wanted is only held back by your own belief systems and your daily practices. It is time to make the change.

The voice inside of you that says "When I grow up, I want to be rich" is right. You can have absolutely everything that you want in this life. Subsequently, you can begin the process of having those things today. You are not bound to where you came from, and you're not even bound to where you are today. Your future has not been decided yet. You get to pick up the pen and write the story of you. You get to ink all the characters. You get to define who you allow inside of your movie. You get to tell the greatest tale that you've ever been told, and you get to be the star.

All you have to do is systematically put yourself in a position of power that allows you to accelerate quicker than those in your surroundings. You have to think it, speak it, and operate as though you couldn't fail if you tried. It is not going to be easy. You are not going to wake up tomorrow and all of a sudden be rich. You are not going to get to plaster the internet with a Lamborghini in the next thirty days. Not responsibly, anyway.

Nevertheless, you are going to have an opportunity to figure out where your gifting is. You are going to have an opportunity to realize your passions. You're going to, like Grandpa said, walk with your eyes open recognizing the opportunities and gaps all around you. You are going to have the skill sets to make whatever life you want a reality.

Yes, the steps are simple! You need to know why you do what you do every day. You need to recognize the people around you for who they are, and make a conscious decision to migrate towards the upper third. You need to surround yourself with the very best mentors that you can. This will be one of the hardest things that you do as an entrepreneur, because you will have to step outside of your comfort zone. You must be humble, and ask for help.

You will have to be diligent enough to pick up a book and read. Reading allows you to give yourself access to the greatest mentors in the world. In addition, listen to an audiobook on your way back and forth to work. You will have to cut loose of the old stories that you've been telling yourself about your childhood. You will have to make a conscious decision to not allow the stories of your past to put you in a box that prevents you from growing into who you were designed to be.

You will have to push yourself physically and mentally, expanding your own belief system and strengthening that voice inside of you that says "We were meant for more than this. We were meant to be rich." Pushing yourself and strengthening that voice are essential elements of growth.

You will have to develop habits that squash that negative voice. You must be compelled to remove those people that enforce the negative voice and its destructive lies. You will have to figure out what your super powers are and what your weak-

nesses are. Additionally, you will leverage the things that you're brilliant at while protecting yourself mindfully of the things that cause you to fall short.

Before you can do any of those things, you've got to be willing to jump. You have to make a decision to make a change. And, please make it today. It has to be real. It has to come from a place inside of you that's fueled by all of the things that I just listed. You can create the greatest movie ever told... Yours.

Savvy?

Note from the Author

I am excited to share with you the practical steps that I have taken to go from being 300K in debt to altering the course of my family's financial future.

Remember, being rich isn't always about money. A close friend recently said something that hit me in the heart. He said, "Maybe the new 'billionaire' is the person who impacts the lives of a billion people."

I want to see you reach your highest potential and crush your dreams! Most importantly I hope you grow into the fullest version of your God given talents and passions to positively impact this world. Go get it!

Savvy?

Best Wishes,

Michael Munsterman